GOD

is not . . .

GOD

is not . . .

Religious, Nice,
"One of Us,"
An American,
A Capitalist

D. Brent Laytham, editor

BrazosPress

Grand Rapids, Michigan

© 2004 by D. Brent Laytham

Published by Brazos Press
a division of Baker Book House Company
P.O. Box 6287, Grand Rapids, MI 49516-6287
www.brazospress.com

Printed in the United States of America

Library of Congress Cataloging-in-Publication Data
D. Brent Laytham
    God is not—: religious, nice, "one of us," an American, a capitalist / [edited by] D. Brent Laytham.
        p.   cm.
    Includes bibliographical references and index.
    ISBN 1-58743-101-7 (pbk.)
    1. God. 2. United States—Religion. I. Laytham, D. Brent. II. Laytham, D. Brent. III. Laytham, D. Brent.
    BT103.G62 2004
    231—dc22   2003025188

CONTENTS

ACKNOWLEDGMENTS

This book began at North Park University as a series of forums sponsored by the Institute for Christianity, Faith, and Culture during the 2002–2003 academic year. Thanks to provost Margaret Haefner for envisioning the campus theme program, to Don Wagner for chairing the work of the Institute, and to the indefatigable efforts of Jen Pope, whose administrative skill is the reason that these forums went so smoothly. North Park librarians Ann Briody and Sally Anderson assisted with reference questions.

Additional thanks go to North Park Theological Seminary, and especially to dean Stephen Graham for the support and encouragement to pursue this project. I was capably assisted along the way by Joe Chung, Andrew Stonina, and Karen Lichleyter-Klein. These latter two, along with my wife, Missy Laytham, have given much help in the tedious work of copy editing, saving us from many errors and infelicities. Missy, Joel Shuman, Steve Long, and Edgardo Colon-Emeric read various portions of the manuscript and offered extremely helpful advice.

Neither the forums nor this book would have been feasible without additional funding provided by the Christian Scholars Lecture Series of the Pew Charitable Trust. I am deeply grateful to Kurt Berends, coordinator of the series, for invaluable advice and encouragement regarding the lectures and their publication. His assistant Debra Dochuk cared for innumerable administrative details that made this project possible.

My gratitude to my five coauthors goes well beyond their contribution here. Their friendship has enriched me for many years. In addition, Mike Budde's work with The Ekklesia Project—whose speakers bureau was the clearinghouse for the original lectures—was the genesis of this project. Rodney Clapp's ongoing vision for Brazos Press and the place this book might find there encouraged me to see it through to the end. Finally, my editor Rebecca Cooper deserves boundless thanks for guiding a green author/editor through his first book.

INTRODUCTION

D. Brent Laytham

Tell Me All Your Thoughts on God

Who is God? This question is easier to ask than to answer. There are a number of reasons for the difficulty, some of which this book will explore. But perhaps one of the greatest difficulties is unexpected. These days we talk about God too easily and too much. In the song "Counting Blue Cars," Dishwalla sings, "Tell me all your thoughts on God, 'cause I would really like to meet her." I enjoy the song, especially the surprising "her." But my response to its central request is "No, please don't; anything but that! You don't tell me 'all your thoughts on God,' and I won't tell you all of mine, either." The incessant chatter of God-talk in contemporary American culture is simply too trite, banal, and pandering to raise our sights to the Source of all truth, beauty, and goodness. To quote a grace said before meals in my childhood, "God is great"—greater even than our ability to speak God's greatness. Thus, one of the goals of this book is to suggest that it is harder to think and speak of God than people normally imagine. Indeed, the authors of the essays will be pleased if readers find themselves struggling to find words that are worthy of God.[1] But the authors' primary goal is to invite readers into the struggle for lives that are worthy of the living God.

The book began when North Park University decided to tackle the question "Who is God?" as a campus dialogue during the 2002–2003 academic year. As I thought about how to answer the question without trivializing God, I was reminded of Thomas Aquinas's startling claim that we cannot know what God is, but only what God is not.[2] Aquinas means to teach us that knowing what "God is not" is not the same as knowing nothing about God. As Aquinas develops the theme, we learn that God is not embodied, God is not material, God is not contained within the world, and so forth. While none of these claims say precisely who or what God is, they do advance our understanding by eliminating false possibilities.

Times change, but knowing what God is not continues to be crucial. In translating Aquinas's strategy of negation from the thirteenth century at the University of Paris to the twenty-first century at North Park University, it seemed to me that today the most important negations were no longer the explicitly philosophical but the implicitly political. Our greatest difficulty in speaking of God comes from the way various communities and allegiances distort our understanding of God. These communities and allegiances include the state, the market, race, class, and gender. Each of them generates powerful practices, disciplines, and attitudes that shape and direct our thoughts and desires. Sometimes we can see clearly where and how this happens—the racialization of God by white supremacists, for example, or the commercialization of God by certain televangelists. But those distortions we recognize easily are usually someone else's problem. The distortions that hold *us* are most often exceedingly difficult to see.

If I am right that these communities and allegiances form a context that distorts our ability to know God, then contesting and critiquing them should help us to know God more truly. That is, we need to learn again to say with Aquinas, "God is not." Toward that end, I developed a series of five "God Is Not" forums that have now become the central chapters of this book. The topic of each forum, and thus the shape of this book, was quite contingent. Rather than try to identify the five most pressing negations, I called upon five friends whose academic work had already engaged cultural-political distortions of God. A more programmatic approach would certainly have required lectures titled "God Is Not Male" and "God Is Not White." Both claims contest key distortions of theology and community in American Christianity. Happily, both claims have been getting serious theological attention for some time now and can be pursued in other essays and books. The theological negations contained in this book, on the other hand, often get far less attention. So this book does not claim to give a comprehensive account of what God is not. It certainly is not "all our thoughts on God." But it does hope to offer key negations of particularly troubling distortions of God, distortions that afflict the church's life and thought to the very core.

Bringing the church into the conversation already suggests that this book is written from Christian conviction.[3] It is. But the book does not assume that such convictions are shared by all readers. Indeed, the arguments here are meant to be accessible to persons of other faiths (or of no faith). Moreover, we hope that such readers will share, or be convinced by, a number of our cultural critiques, historical analyses, and social perceptions. Perhaps discovering shared no's could allow Christians and Jews or Christians and Muslims to explore more effectively the possibility of a shared yes. Perhaps discovering shared no's could allow persons skeptical of Christian faith or repulsed by Christians' conduct to see the God that Christians worship in a new light. Discovering such commonalities might allow persons with different fundamental commitments or communities to say "Well, we agree on this."

We Who?

Stanley Hauerwas regularly reminds us to watch our pronouns, to ask who is included or excluded when we say "we."

He uses a story about the Lone Ranger and Tonto to make the point. Once they "found themselves surrounded by twenty thousand Sioux. The Lone Ranger turned to Tonto and asked, 'What do you think we ought to do, Tonto?' Tonto responded, 'What do you mean by "we," white man?'"[4] "We who?" is a question that desperately needs asking in the church. Readers of this book would do well to ask it of the six authors of this collection: How is this group a "we," and what sort of "we" is it?

We collaborate on this book as a group of friends who find ourselves bound together by common convictions about the Triune God of Christian faith. That is to say, our friendship is not primarily grounded in liking each other, though we generally do, but in knowing that we belong to Jesus Christ in his body, the church. The authors are members of The Ekklesia Project, an organization committed to promoting radical discipleship in local congregations and beyond.[5] The basic principles include 1) allegiance to the Triune God, who in Christ has priority over every competing allegiance; 2) practice of communal worship as the heart of Christian life; 3) resistance to the claims and practices of the culture of death; and 4) efforts to restore the unity of the body of Christ. Because of our common involvement, we have not only read each other's writings, but have prayed and argued and planned and eaten together. In Christ we affirm a unity deeper than the divisions among the various communities to which we belong (the authors include lay and religious Catholics, United Methodists, and an Episcopalian). So unlike in many collections of essays, the "we who?" of this book is a fairly cohesive group with a fairly unified perspective.

Bill Cavanaugh, in "God Is Not Religious," calls this book the theological equivalent of the *Jerry Springer Show*. In one sense, Bill is exactly right: we hope to provoke a reaction, and we present with an over-the-top flair (though we're not going to throw any chairs). But we don't imagine that God will ever make an appearance on *Springer,* because *God is not a scold* and *God is not a boor. God Is Not,* on the other hand, sounds like we could be scornful of what others believe or boorishly self-assertive about our own convictions. We hope not, though not because we're too polite for such ill-mannered behavior. Rather, we believe that we must refuse to play the scold or the boor because of the way our Christian life centers in the church's practice of communion and baptism.

First, communion is more basic than criticism. Criticism—the attempt to analyze and purify Christian thought and action—is an important part of the work of theology. For many Christians, though, this part appears to be the whole. To them, theology seems to be primarily magpie work. The way of the magpie is to sit comfortably overhead while criticizing everyone below. That's what theologians seem to do, perching themselves at an esoteric height, safely above the fray, then chattering incessant criticism at earnest Christians who live and work in the real world. We refuse to play the magpie. Though there are direct and indirect criticisms here, they are never offered from above or beyond. Rather, we live and work and speak in the same real world as everyone else. The criticisms offered here begin with the admission that we, too, have been tempted to think of God as American or a capitalist; we, too, have been tempted to act as if God were nice or religious; we, too, have been captured by the crowd.

Moreover, we recognize that the body of Christ is not constituted by an "above" and a "below," but by a gathering *around* Christ's eucharistic table. Thus we cannot act as if we have no relation to persons who may hold dearly or feel deeply the convictions we deny. Rowan Williams notes how easily a casual comment may strike "at the ground of your faith," so that it "suddenly devalues all your intellectual struggles and puts your integrity into question."[6] Why is this? Because "It's my life you're threatening, my sense and my judgment, my *meaning,* the way I painfully struggle to understand myself in the light of God and the gospel."[7] Like Williams, we know that convictions about God are woven into the very fabric of human life. We also know that, fundamentally different perspectives of God notwithstanding, the Eucharist binds us together irrevocably. Because we recognize this, because we seek continually to recognize Christ in the breaking of the

bread (Luke 24:31), we offer these reflections on God in humility—not to annihilate faith or to annoy the faithful, but
to serve and strengthen the body of Christ.

Which leads to the claim that baptism drowns the boor.
Regardless of what we intend by way of humility and service,
our assertions that "God is not" seem to constitute theological
boorishness. The way of the boor is to rush into the middle,
ignoring social decorum or transgressing accepted etiquette.
So what is the etiquette of talk about God in our day? Phyllis
Tickle suggests that the "rules of conversational good manners in god-talk today in America" include "reverence and
an unflinching tolerance for what others revere with a sworn
unwillingness to discriminate (except for one's own private
use) among all the honored options."[8]

By the standards Tickle reports, then, the God-talk in this
book is boorishly beyond the bounds of good manners. Yet
her rule of theological etiquette rests on the claim that faith
is essentially and absolutely a *private* matter. She names it
"our *privatized* theology *privately* forged" (italics added). Each
person's house brand of theology may be shared, but only
voluntarily and intimately. It may not be "systematized and
dogmatized and organized for us by somebody else, except
perhaps indirectly and then only by an exquisitely courteous
sensibility. Most certainly they may not be—in fact, cannot
credibly be—scrutinized for flaws or inconsistencies by those
in a different divine/human relationship. . . ."[9]

We begin with the premise that Christian conviction is
always public and shared, never a private possession. As
we see it, on Tickle's terms for postmodern God-talk, perhaps nothing is quite so boorish as the church's practice of
baptism. For as traditionally practiced, Christian baptism
is necessarily public, communal, and discriminating. First,
baptism is the *public* incorporation of an individual into a
God-community and its ongoing God-conversation. The
ritual is a visible event in the midst of a specific public—the
community of the baptized. Second, baptism says "no" to our
modern pretensions about being self-sufficient, autonomous
individuals; you cannot baptize yourself! Christian baptism is

always organized by the church and received at the hands of another Christian; in other words, it is a *community* event. So a "privatized theology privately forged" drowns in Paul's baptismal claim that "you are not your own" (1 Cor. 6:19). This means, finally, that baptism is a radical change of allegiance that is inherently *discriminating*. Baptism enacts conversion, a turning away from one way of life (renunciation) and a turning toward God and the way of Christ (adhesion). Because this change of allegiance is so radical, it necessarily requires that we make discriminations about which convictions are compatible with Christ and which are not. Indeed, the first discrimination is that the faith we profess in baptism was the church's before it was ours. Some churches have embodied this necessary discrimination through ritual scrutinies or exorcisms.[10] But even where discriminations are not ritualized, baptism nonetheless *scrutinizes* us in ways antithetical to the "exquisitely courteous sensibility" of modern God-talk that refuses to be "scrutinized for flaws."

In other words, if God is willing to be boorish in baptism, then we'll run that same risk. In the essays that follow, we scrutinize some of the God-talk that is current in the church and the world. But we do this believing that true boorishness is the "unflinching tolerance" that cannot tolerate traditional Christian conviction. The true boors are those who revere and honor all options but the one God has chosen—the church.[11] We are convinced that "through Jesus Christ, we are called to give our allegiance to God and to make the Church our true dwelling place."[12] Therefore, we say "no" to the etiquette of privatized God-talk, not to start a *Springer*-esque shouting match, but to make more clear God's "yes" in Jesus Christ.

God Is Not . . . What?

In "God Is Not 'a Stranger on the Bus'" Rodney Clapp invites us to engage the images of God that inhabit popular culture. Beginning with Joan Osborne's popular single "One of Us," Clapp suggests that the god of this song is "the ideal pop culture deity," not so different from the average consumer of popular culture: a passive spectator carried along by mass culture and technology. Because Christians have been, and are called to be, more critically engaged with culture than that, Clapp suggests that we be particularly wary of the way popular culture engages crowd behaviors. Clapp points to two paradigmatic biblical stories about crowds—the golden calf incident and the crowd's role in the final week of Jesus' ministry—to suggest that crowds all too easily crowd God out.

But crowds don't always exclude or distort God. Luke is at pains to suggest that part of the glory of the day of Pentecost is the large crowd—more than three thousand—who believe the gospel that Peter proclaims (see Acts 2). And the Revelation describes God's grand finale as including a multitude beyond count (Rev. 7:9). Crowds require discernment, and so does the culture of the crowd—popular culture. Clapp recommends a discernment that is not mere evaluation—thumbs up or thumbs down—but instead actively engages popular culture "case by case, practice by practice, artifact by artifact." To assist that engaged discernment, Clapp offers three distinctions. First is Karl Barth's distinction between religion and revelation, which suggests that God's revelation in Jesus Christ is the standard by which we look for God's appearance in popular culture. Second is the distinction between public and community; Clapp suggests that the community called church claims us in a way that public mass media never will. Finally comes the distinction between the opinions that we have and the convictions that have us. Clapp concludes by suggesting that the church's creed about Christ—the Nicene Creed, which embodies the community's convictions on revelation—is a good place to stand, whoever is singing on the radio.

In "God Is Not Nice" Steve Long warns us against the siren song of our therapeutic culture: "God is nice, and he's on your side." Where Clapp focuses on popular culture's fascination with a God like us, Long turns to our insatiable desire for a God who likes us. We long for a nonthreatening, usable deity, one who will boost our self-esteem and our sense of well-being (if not our golf handicap or our stock portfolio). Church leaders—pastors and denominational leaders alike—give us exactly what we want: the nice god, a smiling, malevolent hybrid of the Grand Inquisitor and Mickey Mouse. As Long develops his argument, we come to see that there's nothing quite so dangerous as the nice God.

Escaping the clutches of the nice god requires more than repeating the mantra "God is not nice." It requires first that we learn to recognize the two sources of the sentimentalized deity: our therapeutic culture, which turns pastors into managers and therapists, and the Protestant theological heritage, which confines God to God's usefulness "for me." Second, Long invites us to rediscover the moral and intellectual seriousness of the Triune God. Our guides in the uncharted territory beyond God-is-nice are Thomas Aquinas and Julian of Norwich. Aquinas tells us that God is not really related to us and loves us only because God loves himself. This sounds like really bad news. But in fact, only because God doesn't need us is the fullness of God's love available to us. Julian tells us that, though God is not nice, God is kind. And God's kindness enfolds us so fully that, regardless of life's tragedies, "all shall be well."

The American sense of well-being seemed profoundly shaken by the terrorist attacks of September 11, 2001. In "God Is Not American" Father Michael Baxter writes quite consciously for our post-9/11 world, suggesting that less may have changed than many people think. Baxter begins by noting that the myth of "American exceptionalism" is alive and well after 9/11; the 2002 controversy about the phrase "under God" in the Pledge of Allegiance is simply the latest chapter in the story that the United States is a "Christian nation." It is this story that Baxter challenges. Rather than speak in generalities, Baxter devotes the bulk of his essay to an extended review and critique of the December 2001 editorial, "In a Time of War" by Richard John Neuhaus, that was printed in *First Things*. This strategy works quite well because Neuhaus is such an articulate exponent of the "Christian nation" story. When Baxter demonstrates that Neuhaus's telling of the story makes huge holes in the fabric of truth, it is ample evidence of just how unholy the story itself is.

Baxter first exposes and critiques the editorial's claim that the United States is "a nation under God." To the degree the statement is true, Baxter suggests, the god that the nation is under is not the Triune God. Second, Baxter analyzes Neuhaus's discussion of some ancient Christian advice on citizenship from the *Letter to Diognetus*. Baxter agrees with Neuhaus that the *Letter* is good advice for faithful Christian living. He reveals, however, that by a remarkable infidelity to the actual text of the *Letter to Diognetus*, Neuhaus ends up recommending a remarkable infidelity to the way of life that the *Letter* recommends. This is rooted in Neuhaus's story of "Christian America," a story that calls us to live from a Christian past and for a Christian future in the certain knowledge that the present moment has linked the fate of the nation itself to the fate of Christianity. Neuhaus believes that Christianity is locked in a death struggle with Islam, with the United States being the chief gladiator for the Christian West. In contrast to this disordering of our allegiances, Baxter suggests that we focus on what it means to be "one church under God." The Christian challenge, in times of war or peace, is to pledge and live this allegiance to the one God in the one body of Christ.

Lately, though, the church as body of Christ is being reimagined as the church as business of Christ. On the very day that Michael Budde presented "God Is Not a Capitalist," a *Simpsons* rerun aired in Chicago that had Mr. Burns (the sitcom's stereotypical bottom-line capitalist) taking over the local church to save it from financial ruin. After Burns put advertising on the walls of the sanctuary and inserted commercials into the church announcements, Lisa Simpson declares that she has become a Buddhist. Who needs careful theological argument when you've got dripping social satire from *The Simpsons* (or *The Onion*, from which Budde quotes)?

We do, Budde suggests, precisely because contemporary church and culture continue to confuse God with Warren Buffett or Bill Gates. The first form of this confusion that Budde tracks is the various ways in which the church has sought to operate like a for-profit corporation. "Christianity Incorporated," as Budde calls it, is rampant in the church, and its pervasiveness is due as much to a failure of Christian nerve and vision as it is to the successes of consumer capitalism. The second form of confusion turns Jesus into the epitome of corporate leadership. Budde makes his case by summarizing the *Jesus CEO* phenomenon, Laurie Beth Jones's conversion of Jesus into a "spiritreneur." This is just a particularly egregious example of countless interpretations that suggest that Jesus walked the way of the cross to help the clever businessperson succeed.

To emphasize just how ridiculous these characterizations of Christian faith are, Budde does a bit of satire. He compares the God of Holy Scripture to our common understanding of what counts for good business sense. In the first place, Budde demonstrates that God has a poor business plan—at least, the God portrayed in Jesus' parables should hardly expect to succeed in the marketplace. Moreover, God refuses to adopt the most basic practices of a capitalistic economy; Jesus didn't even charge a fee for his miracles! Budde concludes his biblical survey by moving from satire to sermon. He offers a powerful reinterpretation of the parable of the talents (from Matthew 25), "the parable that most often finds its way into justifications for the harmony of Christianity and capitalism." Budde asks us to take the ruthless owner as the satanic figure that he is, and to take the third servant—the one who wastes it all and is rejected for his failure—as a figure of the servant Jesus, who bankrupts himself on the cross, who is rejected for his failure, who is our help and our hope precisely because he destroys the logic of the market. Budde concludes the essay by inviting the church to read the Sermon on the Mount as a primer in economics. There we find God's abundance depicted as so overwhelming that the church could, if it dared, begin to live in "God's radical economy."

One thing is certain, God's economy is neither personal nor private. Unfortunately, too many well-meaning people think that their relationship with God is. Who among us hasn't heard a celebrity or acquaintance say, "I'm a very spiritual person, but I'm not religious"? The implication is that God might not be too different. Imagine God confiding to Letterman or Leno,

"I'm a very spiritual God, but lately I'm just not very religious."
Such a hip God would clearly approve the sentiment in a recent
book title *More Jesus, Less Religion.*[13] At first glance, this might
appear to be the sentiment implied by Bill Cavanaugh's "God
Is Not Religious." In fact, however, Cavanaugh suggests that
the "religious versus spiritual" choice is a false one, since both
adjectives have a similar effect: confining God to part, rather
than all, of human life.

To make his case, Cavanaugh takes us on a fascinating journey with the word "religion," showing that its connection with
Christianity is a relatively recent one. It corresponds almost
exactly with the emergence of the modern nation-state, and
Cavanaugh suggests that this connection is not accidental.
Rather, religion has functioned to show God the door, clear-
ing space for the demands of nation and market for ultimate
allegiance. In the process, he says, ". . . the term 'religion' has
been part and parcel of the trivialization of God in our society."
The living God calls Christians not to be religious, but to center
their lives in the church and its practices of worship, witness,
and service. In other words, Christians will be visible because
of the (specifically Christian) things that they do.

Cavanaugh then details how the rise of religion has worked
to interiorize, privatize, and relativize Christian life. First,
religion drives Christianity out of the visible world into an
individual's head or heart; Christians become mere believers,
no longer behavers. Once Christians have God "buried deep in
the recesses of the individual heart," it is a small second step
to make Christian commitment a private matter. Because the
private is necessarily contrasted with the public, the limitation of Christianity to the private realm clears a public space
for other communities and commitments. In other words,
at best, religion allows God to rule hearts and minds but not
bodies; bodies belong to other powers—armies or corporations. At worst, religion becomes a "private leisure activity";
some people like Canasta, some like scuba diving, some like
church. Finally, religion becomes religions, and the gospel
becomes simply one choice among many paths to God. Thus,
in our day the concept of religion works to make Christian life

something not only inner and private, but now relative as well. Cavanaugh's chapter is a clarion call to "lose our religion," to stop using religion to avoid God. The result may not make us more spiritual, but it will surely invite the church to more "boldly proclaim the sovereignty of God over all creation."

In "God Is One, Holy, Catholic, and Apostolic," I seek to do three things. First, I summarize the logic of the prior chapters by suggesting that speaking of God will always require great care with language, neither claiming to say neither more nor less than we are able. Thomas Aquinas's discussion of analogy offers assistance here. Second, I summarize the way contemporary culture complicates our speaking of God by looking at the first three commandments of the Decalogue. We are constantly tempted to have God à la carte (rather than have no other gods), or to put God in orbit around other commitments (rather than refuse graven images), or to assume that our names for God are human constructions (rather than divine gifts).

Finally, I return to the relationship of church to God. When we profess belief in the "one, holy, catholic, and apostolic Church" (Nicene Creed), we are in fact suggesting that the church is these things only because God is. If the world is ever to see truly who God is and what God is not, it requires that the church visibly enact these marks by faithful practice. I conclude by suggesting that there are specific activities that God has given the church that mark God's unity, holiness, catholicity, and apostolicity.

In a comment on Israel's praise during the exile, Walter Brueggemann epitomizes what this entire book seeks to convey about who God is, what God is not, and the difference it makes:

> The naming of the name in the new song is a polemic. For every time the name is sung, some other pretender is dismissed. The affirmation of Yahweh always contains a polemic against someone else. Thus in its song, Israel might say:
> Yahweh and not Baal.
> Yahweh and not Dagon.

Yahweh and not Marduk.
Yahweh and not Zeus.
Yahweh and not Hobbes, not Adam Smith, not George
    Gilder.
Yahweh and not any pseudo-power.
. . . The song dares to say . . . "only Yahweh—none of
    the above."[14]

Like the "none of the above" that goes with "only Yahweh,"
surely there is a "God is not" that goes with "Jesus is Lord."

— 1 —

God Is Not "A Stranger on the Bus"

Discerning the Divine in Popular Culture

Rodney Clapp

In 1995, the bluesy rock singer Joan Osborne released a song called "One of Us." Given its popularity and pervasiveness, you are likely to remember it. Straightforwardly theological, the song's most famous refrain asked,

> What if God was one of us
> Just a slob like one of us

Just a stranger on the bus
Trying to make his way home?

If you are like me, you might answer that if God is one of us, as lost and clueless as we are, then we really are in trouble. But that is not the response the songwriter designs to elicit. The song teases and entices us with the prospect of a god who is like us, only more so. For our day, this is the ideal pop culture deity: a god who is not in control, not directing history in any real sense. This god does not drive, but only rides the bus in a befuddled funk, trying to figure out the maze of mass transportation from flat maps and soulless guidebooks rendered by faceless bureaucrats. Borne along, this god watches the sights flitting by the window, presumably alternately amused and appalled like all the other passengers. This deity is nothing more than a spectator, a passive observer. Furthermore, and again true to the popular culture of our day, this deity changes faces, is always a stranger and nondescript slob. Like the celebrities that modern, mass-media popular culture endlessly generates, gobbles up, and discards, this god takes on an unending and indeterminate succession of disguises or appearances. In other words, this malleable and shape-shifting god is always who "we" want god to be. This god has an identity and character as fluid as rock music charts, Nielsen ratings, and public-opinion polls.

With this lead-in, you may expect that what follows is a rant by a hater of popular culture. But that is not the case, so I am hastening to some definitions. By *culture* I mean a social body and process that forms particular sorts of persons. Culture is both discourse and practices, a formational way of life. Culture *cultivates*—taking raw, unshaped human beings, it seeds and nurtures and prunes them. It cultivates particular kinds of persons by constructing their perception of their experience, of life, the world, what they will know as reality. Culture gives us language, categories, narratives, and other organizational schemes by which we make sense of ourselves and everything we meet. Human beings are social creatures, and culture is what informs and transforms our identity and vision.

Popular culture, then, is the culture of the broad populace, the people. It is not confined to elites, such as aristocrats or college professors. Nor is it segregated only to "high" times and places, such as classical music in the concert hall, where people gather for a special event and sit reverently and quietly to attend the tuxedoed orchestra. Popular culture wears blue jeans and hits the streets. Popular culture is the culture of the everyman and the everyday.

In these regards, unless you despise ordinary people and everyday life, it makes no sense to monolithically oppose popular culture. Aren't we all, at least much of the time and in many ways, ordinary? And how can any of us escape the quotidian rhythms of mundane existence? More importantly, there are profound theological reasons for us Christians to affirm popular culture. We profess that the God met in Israel and Jesus Christ made all creatures and creation, and pronounced them and it good. Moreover, this God holds a special place in God's heart for slaves and plebeians, for strangers and sojourners, for people poor and otherwise parenthetical—that is, people put in the parentheses of life's sentences and easily overlooked or forgotten.

Given all this, the church has eagerly translated Holy Scripture into the "vulgar" or common language of various peoples.[1] In fact, the central Christian conviction of the incarnation profoundly grounds the church's historical willingness to translate Scripture into a vast variety of spoken and written languages. The incarnation affirms that God, in the person and work of Jesus of Nazareth, entered history and supremely revealed God's self and God's purposes for the world. Jesus the Christ, both divine and human, deigned to redeem the world through and in a specific time and culture (first-century Palestinian Judea). Jesus, as the Apostles' Creed has it, "suffered under Pontius Pilate"—he accomplished his saving work through a specific, messy, nitty-gritty, and literally bloody history. So the incarnation itself is a divine "translation" into a certain culture, not just "culture" or "history" or "the cosmos" in general (whatever that might or even could mean).

Following what might be called the logic of the incarnation, then, the Christian can marvel at and praise specific, actual culture of many sorts, including the most common or ordinary. Saint Augustine, for example, can wax positively rhapsodic about the glories of human culture. He carries on in awe about clothing, architecture, agriculture, navigation, pottery, painting, music, literature, and medicine. He revels in the gustatory pleasures of seasonings and spices and culinary methods. He is swept away by the wondrous explorations of what we would now call the natural sciences, exclaiming, "How abundant is man's stock of natural phenomena! It is beyond description. . . ." He can recall with pleasant fascination a man who could wiggle his ears without touching them, and even one who could fart on tune. Augustine does not stop appreciating human ingenuity, the ambiguous beauty and scintillation of its contrivances, even when that ingenuity is turned to evil purposes such as "weapons of prisons and wars," "theatrical spectacles," and heresy. Though surely no friend of heretics, he acclaims "the brilliant wit shown by the philosophers and heretics in defending their very errors and falsehoods [as] something which beggars imagination!"[2]

But there are aspects of popular culture as we now know it that I think merit a more critical attitude, and even suspicion. Modern popular culture is predominately mediated. It comes to us through the mass media, as songs and films and television programs already created and prepackaged. At the beginning of the twentieth century, the most widely practiced form of popular music was indicated by the prolific sales of sheet music. Although most amateur musicians did not write their own music, they did actively interpret it at the piano in the parlor or with the guitar on the front porch. Family members and other listeners who might not themselves have mastered a musical instrument were, nonetheless, directly involved in the music's interpretation and rendition. "Play more quietly and serenely," they might say to the son or daughter at the keyboard. Or, to the guitarist or fiddler who was a sister or neighbor: "Not so slow and sad. Lift our spirits with it, won't you?"

By comparison, professionally produced and corporately distributed CDs and radio stations incline their listeners to a more passive attitude, like that of the spectator-passenger on a bus. Modern popular culture is in large part mass, and mass-mediated, culture. It is, in its production, removed from particular communities and their specific creation or engagement. It is commodified and calls us to treat it like a drug, to simply pay for it and swallow or "consume" it. And like a drug, it is expected to deaden our pain or boredom, or to arouse and exhilarate us without any effort and active engagement on our part. We climb on the bus of this popular culture and sit down to fall into a torpor, expecting to doze complacently and open our eyes at intervals only to be entertained and distracted. With it we "veg out" and drift, voyeurs carried past endless oddities on the other side of the screen that is our window onto life. Then we gorge and fall asleep until the next scandal or novelty appears. We measure or evaluate any instance or artifact of this popular culture only by the numbers among the masses who momentarily find their attention arrested by it. "Good" or "successful" popular culture, in these terms, is simply the movie the most people saw last weekend, or the CD bought this week by more teenagers than any other, or the news show the largest number of Americans turn on tonight.

On Crowding God Out

To assess this state of affairs theologically, I want to begin by recalling two biblical stories. The first is the story of Israel's construction of the golden calf (found in Exodus 32). The people wander in the wilderness and camp at the base of Mount Sinai. Moses ascends the mountain to learn from God what shape Israel's legal and political system will take. Moses deputizes his brother Aaron to watch the store while he is away. When Moses has not returned to camp for some time, the people grow impatient and insecure. Moses represented the God who led them out of Egypt; now Moses is gone and perhaps dead. The people must be reassured they remain a unified people and have a future, which is but to say that they need a god. Aaron is altogether accommodating. He collects and melts golden earrings, and fashions a golden calf. Later Moses returns to find the people reveling around their idol, the gold bull, and both his wrath and the wrath of God fall on the people.

The second biblical story to recall is that of the people's demeanor in Jesus' final days. The Messiah enters Jerusalem to great popular acclaim and excitement.[3] Eschewing the irony of his entrance on the back of a humble donkey, the crowd waves palm fronds and throws cloaks in his path. They see what they want to see: a conquering Jewish king come to lead them in an eviction of the hated, colonizing Romans. A mere three days later, on the Festival of the Passover, the Roman Pilate leads the now arrested and mute Jesus before the crowds. In Luke's Gospel account, Pilate tries three times to get the masses to agree to release Jesus. In response, they three times scream for his crucifixion (Luke 23:4–22).

What might these two accounts suggest about God and the masses? Can God be crowded out? I have four suggestions:

(1) The mass, or crowd, can take on a life of its own. Aaron, usually a trusty second to Moses, answers the crowd's call for a manufactured god promptly. When he is confronted by Moses, Aaron stammers that the people demanded the bull, then pleads: "So I said to them, 'Whoever has gold, take it off'; so they gave it to me, and I threw it into the fire, and out came this calf" (Exod. 32:24)! In other words, Aaron never really planned or deliberately intended for this to happen. Somehow the mob and the mob's will took on a life of its own, and poof!—the idol appeared. The mass seems magically irresistible. Again returning to Luke's account of Jesus' final days, Luke—in a way neither Matthew nor Mark does—makes the crowd at the triumphal entry a "multitude of disciples" (Luke 19:37). So Luke suggests these people who so soon turn on the Christ are not just idle thrill-seekers, but followers of Christ. Even Peter the Rock betrays the Lord and seeks simply to blend in with the crowd that will soon demand his death (Luke 22:54–62).

(2) The crowd is fickle but vehement. The Israelites escaping Egypt have seen great deeds at the hand of the God who speaks to Moses. But, especially in the surge of mass excitement, they can quickly forget all that. Once the bull stands, they fall to worship it passionately and revel before it (Exod. 32:6). Likewise, I have already noted that the crowds greeting Jesus triumphantly changed their loyalties inside seventy-two hours. They cry for Christ's death as insistently and with as much abandon as they, not long before, greeted him as king. The bluntest, most indiscriminate motivations move crowds. Gross ecstasy or fear sweeps along everything in its path. Crowds, as crowds, do not stop and think. They are incapable of imagining alternatives and possibilities beyond the present passion, which wholly possesses them.

(3) The crowd creates gods in its own image. The bull was the most powerful animal known to the ancient Israelites. It symbolized power and fertility—brute, majestic, *natural* strength. This was the same natural potency flowing through human veins, so that the people could claim it as their own. Thus the bull signifies the "essence of the people's power as a people, of the mystery of its existence and continuance, of the demonstration of its being as deriving from the tribes themselves, of joy in its own present and the ideal of its future. The bull is for Israel 'a god who understands it and in whom it understands itself.'"[4] And in the Gospels the crowds respond to Jesus when they think he will give them what they already want, that he will represent a god determined to serve their needs. In John's Gospel, the Lord explicitly recognizes as much. After multiplying bread to feed the masses, Jesus challenges the crowd that pursues him: "Very truly, I tell you, you are looking for me, not because you saw signs [of the true God], but because you ate your fill of the loaves" (John 6:26). Finally, Jesus is perceived as the conquering military leader the crowd wants rather than the lamb who will conquer, not by killing, but by himself dying. To put it in modern psychological language, crowds project their wishes or their fears onto given objects. The selfsame person who is today's hero may be tomorrow's scapegoat.

(4) The *vox populi* (voice of the people) should by no means be identified with the *vox Dei* (voice of God). The voice of the insecure Israelites, swept up in the uncontrollable power and vehemence of its mass, falsely proclaims the bull to be god. The voice of the people in the Gospels changes within a few days. As the Gospels (especially Mark) emphasize throughout, Jesus' true identity is not easily discerned and he is frequently ascribed a mistaken identity, not least by unreflective crowds. God and God's ways are revealed publicly but surprisingly when Christ is lifted up on a cross; yet God is seen there only by those with discerning eyes and ears (John 3:14; 8:28).

The Crowd and "Religion"

In sum, fifty million Elvis fans can be wrong. So can two million Nazis, or half a million Leninists, or a majority of Americans. Whether moved trivially, or seriously and lethally, the mass can take on a life for which none of its inhabitants would singly claim responsibility. The mass changes its "mind" easily and rapidly, but acts immediately with overwhelming passion. The mass looks for what it most elementally wants or dreads, and finds that wherever it will. And, whatever we may be tempted to think in the midst of modern declared democracies, God's will is not known by majority vote—especially not the majority vote of unreflective masses.

I think we may helpfully theologically scrutinize mass behavior and "popular opinion" by framing it within Karl Barth's famous critique of "religion." Barth defined religion as "man's attempts to justify and sanctify himself before a capricious and arbitrary picture of God."[5] Rather than interpret and perceive the world through the Christ who is God's revelation to the world, humanity with religion attempts to construct and tell its own story. Religion, whenever it occurs—and Barth argues that the Christian church itself must acknowledge its own unceasing religiousness—is human intent seeking divine rationale.[6] Religion remakes and recasts "God" for a series of human projects and goals. This explains why, though it ostensibly refers to the transcendent and the eternal, religion morphs and takes many forms. As the construct of historical and contingent creatures, religion may and does change. It is "conditioned by nature and climate, by blood and soil, by the economic, cultural, political, in short, the historical circumstances in which [the human religionist] lives." So religion is a matter of "variable" habit and custom. "Nature and climate, or the understanding and technique with which he masters them, may change. Nations and individuals may move. Races may mix. Historical relationships as a whole are found to be in perhaps a slow or a swift but at any rate a continual rate of flux."[7]

Astutely, then, Barth sees religion not primarily as an individual project but a cultural endeavor. A people or "tribe" believes itself to epitomize true humanity. It accordingly yearns to be self-justified and self-sanctified. The individuals within a culture or tribe identify and esteem themselves as members of it. Speaking out of and for their culture, individuals insist it is especially blessed and anointed by "God." Examples are not hard to come by. Think of the many cultural practices that once operated with passionate religious justification, but that we would now readily condemn—practices such as slavery or genocide or the burning of widows on their dead husbands' funeral pyres. Think of the many, many armies that have marched onto fields of battle, with every one claiming "God" was uniquely on its side. In the Middle Ages, the phenomenon of different territories adapting their religion to the will of the prince was so common that a Latin proverb developed: *cuius regio eius religio*—"as goes the sovereignty, so goes the worship."[8] Nor is such thinking confined to the distant past. Consider a cartoonist's recent and all-too-accurate spoofing of the imagined George W. Bush "White House Hymnal." It bears the title, "God Bless America (But Please, No One Else)," and includes such selections as "America, America, God Shed His Grace on Me and Whoever I Say."[9]

Against the recurrent human impulse to sanctify ourselves, the one and true God shows God's self at God's initiative. This God engages Israel and acts decisively through the life, work, death, and resurrection of Jesus Christ. It is from the standpoint of this revelation, Barth says, that "religion is clearly seen to be a human attempt to anticipate what God in His revelation wills to do and does do. It is the attempted replacement of the divine work by a human manufacture. The divine reality offered and manifested to us in revelation is replaced by a concept of God arbitrarily and willfully evolved by man." And: "'Arbitrarily and willfully' here means by his own means, by his own human insight and constructiveness and energy."[10]

How, then, does religion relate to popular culture? Those discourses and practices we would call religions certainly go deeper and are more profound than the passing whims of the masses. Religions are of course capable of fostering reflection and conviction. Yet popular culture purveys and instantiates religion, as well as various religious and quasi-religious impulses. Joan Osborne's song is an especially transparent pop-culture exhibit of religion as Barth defines and criticizes it: God just is "one of us."

Now "culture" and "popular" are both big, capacious words: pop culture is not only about religion as a human project of self-justification. I contend no more than that popular culture includes such religious elements. Further, modern and post-modern popular culture, to repeat, is heavily mass-mediated and commodified. In its mass-mediated and commodified forms, it appeals especially to the crowd. And remember that the crowd's characteristics include a tendency to take on a life of its own, overwhelming the considered judgment and stifling the imagination of the individuals and communities who comprise it. The crowd is fickle and has a short attention span, but it is consistently vehement about its flavor of the day. The crowd casts "God" in its own image and equates the *vox populi* with the *vox Dei*.

In such manner the crowd, the mass, represents in the most immediate, irresponsible, and fleeting ways the worst impulses and features of religion as Barth describes it. The crowd is self-justifying and assumes the righteousness of the cause and god it serves at any given moment. The crowd is arbitrary and capricious, and it can act just as passionately against a cause or person as it did in favor of a cause or person not long before. Motivated by the grossest, simplest, most elemental dreams and dreads, the crowd is easily manipulated by demagogues or demagogic techniques.

But pay attention. For all the fury and vigor of his critique of religion, Barth did not simply dismiss or condemn it. Nor should we simply dismiss or condemn the impulses and manifestations of popular culture, even mass popular culture. The God met in Israel and Christ does not stand aloof from the world and its peoples and all the flux and vicissitudes of their days. In his "revelation God has actually entered a sphere in which His own reality and possibility are encompassed by a sea of more or less adequate . . . parallels and analogies in human realities and possibilities."[11] We may and should look for "parallels and analogies" to God and God's ways in human cultures—popular culture and crowds included. But we must take care to make the lead and controlling factor in any analogy God's God-initiated revelation in Jesus Christ, not the invention of religion or popular culture. What is crucial is that "religion [or popular culture] is understood in the light of revelation," rather than "revelation in the light of religion [or popular culture]."[12]

Among other things, this means the church cannot accept contemporary popular culture's terms for evaluating itself and its events or artifacts. As I mentioned earlier, modern popular culture judges its success, and its excellence, by the numbers. If large numbers are carried along by this recording or film or politician, that recording or film or politician is—at least for the moment—excellent. By contrast, and like Barth making revelation the controlling factor in our analogizing and evaluation, theologian Ellen Charry defines Christian excellence differently:

> Christian excellence comes from a status given from God. . . .
> Excellence comes from learning what God has done on a grand public scale that sets one's life in a fresh context and gives it new direction and meaning. Christian identity is first acknowledged and then chosen, so to speak. One acknowledges God's work,

then decides to live by it. . . . Christian excellence involves an exchange of orientation, loyalty, and focus in life that Paul calls enslavement: putting oneself at the disposal of, and being directed by, God.[13]

So Christian excellence is defined first and finally not in light of religion but of revelation. Christian excellence comes only from "listening" (to God's prior Word and act) before we ourselves undertake "speaking." Nor is our "listening" done once and for all, so that, say, after baptism we are done with listening (to God) and spend all our time speaking. The depth and riches of God's Word are too great to absorb even in a lifetime—we will have cause to listen in wonder through all eternity. Furthermore, history and our lives are always unfolding, taking new and unexpected directions. Day to day and year to year, we must return to God's revelation, God's preceding Word and words, to know how to embody Christian excellence on this particular day, in this given year and place.

Toward More Active Discernment

What this entails is that the Christian engagement of popular culture must genuinely be an engagement. Popular culture is neither monolithically malignant nor monolithically benign. Christians must engage it case by case, practice by practice, artifact by artifact. Or, to put it less abstractly, we must engage it movie by movie, political initiative by political initiative, artist by artist. Furthermore, we need not assume crowds or mass opinion are always bad or misguided. At the *parousia* (the return of Christ), the multitudes of heaven and earth will, with a sound "like many waters" and "mighty thunder-peals," cry out praises to the God known in Israel and Christ (Rev. 19:6–8). The people, the tribes and masses, will present to the Lamb "the glory and the honor of the nations" (Rev. 21:24–27). In other words, there is much that is good and redeemable in the cultures of the masses, much that at the consummation they can present to glorify and honor the Lord of Lords.[14] And, like the angelic hosts already gathered in heaven, they can celebrate God and God's victory en masse—as a community of cultures. This multitude roaring like a waterfall is surely a crowd. But it is not just any old crowd. It is a crowd that sees Christ truly, for what he is; it is a crowd whose members are shaped and formed first and foremost by revelation, not religion.

How, then, are we made fit to join that crowd? We are made fit by baptism and induction into the body of Christ. I said at the outset that culture is a social body and a process that forms particular sorts of persons. The church is that social body that, by the empowerment of the Holy Spirit, enacts the process that forms Christians. The church hands down the language, narratives, and practices by which we are made and come to know ourselves as adoptees into the family of God. If a culture is a social body of perception and imagination, the church is that culture in which we learn to perceive the God who will work in us to "accomplish abundantly far more than all we can ask or imagine" (Eph. 3:20).

What I am talking about is, in a word, discernment. We do, as Christians or any other sort of people, partake of popular culture. Our participation in popular culture is not always a heavy or profoundly significant act. Sometimes, as Freud protested, a cigar is just a cigar, and a momentary distraction is just a momentary distraction. But popular culture, even if only by thousands of small increments and repetitions, does habituate and seriously take a hand in forming us. If you ride the bus passively, you will either get lost or go around in circles. If you ride the bus discerningly, you may get where you need to go. There are two distinctions that may especially help us in an active discernment of modern, mass-mediated popular culture.

The first is a distinction between the "public" and the "community." As should be clear, when I advise ongoing and case-by-case discernment of popular culture, I am not advising discernment undertaken by the isolated, solitary individual. The "self-made" and self-determining man or woman is an illusion, an illusion created by the particular culture that is modern, affluent, highly technologized Western culture.

Christian discernment of popular culture is most faithful and effective when it is consciously social or communal, drawing on the various gifts of various members of the body. So Christian discernment and its outworkings are public in the sense that they are social processes and they are generally not hidden or private.

But there is another sense of "public," especially powerful in our age, of which we should be more wary. That sense is the public as a great mass, a people "apart from any personal responsibility or belonging."[15] Public buildings, spaces, and objects belong to everyone in general and so do not really belong to anyone in particular. Think of the bag of beer cans dumped along the highway, or the filth and ugly graffiti in the restroom at a roadside park. These spaces are "public" and perceived as belonging to nobody. As a rule, we do not foul our own nests, but attitudes and deportment of responsibility and belonging are difficult to inspire or connect in the faceless masses of the modern public.[16] So our sense of belonging and responsibility, and with it the formation of our character, will never be too deep or profound at this "public" level.

We will instead be most profoundly and importantly formed and transformed in community if we understand a community as a people who "belong to one another and to their place."[17] Within community we know and are known. Within community we belong and are held responsible, just as we hold others responsible. The only way to resist the ever-shifting whims and passions of the nondiscriminating public is within a vital community. Again, for Christians that community is the church. And it is worth noting how the church uniquely constitutes a "public" that is a community of communities. After all, a community itself can all too easily fall prey to self-idolizing impulses if it is insular and segregated from other communities. But the church is that social body wherein Christ is equally, wholly present both in all its parts and in its whole. When a congregation or parish partakes of the Eucharist, it partakes of the whole Christ, not merely a fragment or portion of Christ. So it is always linked to other congregations and parishes, to the church catholic. This means that a local

church in America, for instance, cannot ignore the welfare of a
local church in Britain, or in Iraq—whatever popular national
passions currently rage across the land.

The second distinction I want to urge is that between "opinion" and "conviction." Like the public will they can express,
opinions are beliefs held without a deep sense of belonging
or responsibility. Opinions may and often do change rapidly
and repeatedly, as with the direction of the wind. They may be
professed out of a bank of some genuine knowledge, but can
also be posited out of considerable or total ignorance. So, for
instance, when a public opinion poll asks, "Who is to blame for
the explosion of the space shuttle *Columbia*?" the answer tells
us nothing about who or what is actually at fault.[18] We as the
anonymous and general "public" know more about Captain
Kirk's starship *Enterprise* than we know about the *Columbia*
and its operations. If asked such a question, we respond out
of vague impressions, exposure to striking but decontextual-
ized images, and preexisting predilections. Opinions are cheap
and come easy.

A conviction, on the other hand, is a "persistent belief"
that "cannot be relinquished without making its holder a significantly different" person or community.[19] Our convictions
define us. They are beliefs we hold as highly probable or even
certain, out of some considerable experience and reflection. To
change a conviction is to change as a person, to fundamentally
alter an identity—to no longer be an atheist or a communist
or a Christian. So convictions are costly and come hard. Ask
a NASA engineer or someone widowed by the tragedy who is
to blame for the *Columbia* disaster, and you will hear convictions rather than mere opinions.

Accordingly, as a discerning community engaging popular
culture, we do well to cultivate and pay attention to our convictions. It is of course no simple matter to encapsulate the
core convictions of the Christian faith, but the Nicene Creed
is pretty good for a start. These are the convictions, the costly
beliefs, that we need to know and live, and from which we can
then evaluate popular opinion on any given subject. When
we do not know and make our convictions primary, we are

all too apt to be swept up in the passions of the moment and the mass. Very often we regret it in the morning.

Plenty of popular culture can stand up to, and even be enhanced by, active engagement and alert discernment. Christians will engage and discern most faithfully and effectively out of community and conviction. Then we will be less likely to join murderous crowds or be taken in by a lot of bull—gold or otherwise. And then we will sing Joan Osborne's song a bit differently, with something like this final chorus:

> What if Jesus was one of us
> But also God unlike all of us
> Just the Messiah on a cross
> Trying to make his world whole?

—— 2 ——

God Is
Not Nice

D. Stephen Long

"This is God . . . have a nice day!"
          (bookmark for sale on Yahoo!)

"I am the Lord your God . . .
     you shall have no other gods before me."
                    (Exod. 20:2–3)

You can purchase the "nice god" for $1.50 at yahoo.com, plus shipping and handling. The living God of Jewish and Christian faith will cost you considerably more. As Dietrich Bonhoeffer put it, "when Christ calls a man, he bids him come and die." Though these two gods are often confused with one another, though they are regularly called by the same names, they are utterly distinct. The nice god who seeks to meet our every need and who constantly seeks to relate to us on our own terms is not even distantly related to the Triune God of traditional Christian teaching. Yet in contemporary worship, preaching, and teaching, it is regularly the nice god we encounter. This is true in mainline Protestant congregations, where we might expect it. But it is also true in evangelical and suburban Catholic churches, where we might have expected loyalty to the church's Scripture or the church's tradition to inoculate against a trivialized deity.

In this essay I contrast these two images of God in order to show how the contemporary church has been led astray—indeed, led into slavery—by the nice god. The contrast, I confess, is overdrawn. For if the options were as easily seen as I present them here—either the nice god or the Triune God—then there would be less temptation to follow the nice god. But because the nice god continually hides under the cloak of traditional Christian language and practice, because the nice god continually makes alliance with our most passionate pieties and beliefs, I must intentionally overdraw the contrast so that we can see what is difficult to see.

The argument will develop in three stages. First, the nice god is dangerous because he is false—a creation of well-meaning but misguided church leaders, and because he is malicious—intent on killing us by stealth and sentimentality. Second, the nice god is relatively new, produced by the unholy alliance between a therapeutic culture that wants to feel better and a Protestant theology that focuses on Christ's benefits "for us." Third, I will conclude that the nice god, whose only job is to be nice to us, is not as morally or intellectually serious as the Triune God of traditional Christian faith, who always has been and always will be a community of love among the Father, Son, and Holy Spirit. Only this God is fully and finally worthy of our thought and desire, of our worship, service, and praise.[1]

Warning: The Nice God Isn't

"User-Friendly Worship," "Entertainment Evangelism," "Meeting My Spiritual Needs," "The Friendly Church," "Jesus as My Personal Lord and Savior"—whether you find yourself in an evangelical, a mainline Protestant, or even a suburban Catholic church, language like this dominates the contemporary church jargon. Such talk is intended to be inoffensive. What could be less threatening than a god who only seeks my spiritual fulfillment, who wants to meet my needs in a tolerant, inclusive, nonjudgmental style? What could be less threatening than a god who seeks to be my *personal* Savior?" Such talk is intended to be inviting. How are we going to have effective church growth if we do not begin "where people are" by trying to meet their needs? Don't we need first to tell people "God loves you and has a wonderful plan for your life" before we tell them that "following Jesus will lead you to the cross"?

Listen carefully to most children's sermons, and the gospel you hear proclaimed is "God is nice. You should be nice, too." To which the clever child should respond, "Let me get this straight. Jesus was crucified for saying that God is nice and we can be, too?" This problem isn't confined to children's sermons in Protestant churches, though. A Jewish school posts thoughts about God by its third graders, including "I think God is . . . very nice and does nice things for people."[2] An average sermon or homily for the adults is just as likely to suggest that God's primary attribute is being nice—or equivalents like being easy to get along with, helpful in a crisis, or useful on a daily basis.[3] Imagine the extreme makeover this would give Isaiah's vision of God: ". . . I saw the Lord sitting on a lawn chair, close and friendly; and the emblem of his ballcap said Chicago Cubs [readers should fill in their favorite team name here]. Seraphs . . . called to one another and said: 'Nice, nice, nice is the Lord of hosts; the whole earth is full of his niceness'" (Isa. 6:1–3, altered a little).

Why has the church's understanding of God been reduced to this basic doctrine that "God is nice"? Because we want a harmless god. After all, the idea of god appears to have done a great deal of harm in human history. People kill and die in the name of god. In the name of god came the Crusades, the conquest of the Americas, the so-called Wars of Religion. The fact that people will kill and die in the name of their god proves just how dangerous the idea of god is. Many people think that the path to peace requires that we forget about absolutes like god and religion; think "Imagine" by John Lennon. But since some people cannot break the god habit altogether, the next best thing is to at least domesticate God in order to curb the danger.

Taming God sounds like the work of people outside the church, people who don't really believe in God or take the Bible seriously. But taking the Bible seriously is harder than it sounds, because the biblical God can be dangerous. Take the earliest story of ordination to the priesthood. When Moses was on the mountain receiving the Ten Commandments, the people grew impatient and fashioned a god for themselves—a golden calf. When Moses came down and saw what had happened, he was outraged. He asked, "Who is on the Lord's side? Come to me!" Only the sons of Levi went to his side. And Moses said, "Thus says the Lord, the God of Israel, 'Put your sword on your side, each of you! Go back and forth from gate to gate throughout the camp, and each of you kill your brother, your friend and your neighbor.'" And when they had done this, Moses said, "Today you have ordained yourselves for the service of the Lord, each one at the cost of a son or a brother, and so have brought a blessing on yourselves this day" (Exod. 32:26–29). This is ordination to the service of the Lord? Now that is not nice!

What kind of God allows his name to be used for that kind of despicable act? The golden calf never commanded such carnage. It offered the people spiritual fulfillment and a good time, too. When the golden calf was worshiped, the people "rose early the next day, and offered burnt-offerings and brought sacrifices of well-being; and the people sat down to eat and drink, and rose up to revel" (Exod. 32:6). A god who invites you to rise up and revel is a god who clearly wants to satisfy your personal "needs." Today we call this "entertainment evangelism" and suggest that faithful congregations adopt its strategies.[4] But this God in whose name Moses speaks, this God seems dangerous—especially since this particular story is not an isolated incident. Surely that is why we try to domesticate the dangerous God of Israel and Christianity into an image, a concept, a "god" that we can more easily contain. We seek a god who will not allow for this kind of frightening excess. A god who is . . . nice.

But beware the nice god with the saccharine smile; beneath lies a vindictive spirit. Of course, the nice god appears to be fairly innocuous. His purpose is to give us a good time while insuring that god can never be taken so seriously as to demand that we sacrifice or suffer, that we die or kill in his name. It sounds like a safe strategy. But turning the living God into a sentimental idea does not make God less dangerous; it only hides the danger. And the danger is hidden even more by the fact that the primary purveyors of this kinder, gentler god are those who bear authority in the church. The nice god wants to kill us, but we can't see it because he is presented by a clericalism that is a monstrous hybrid of the Grand Inquisitor and Mickey Mouse.

Fyodor Dostoevsky introduces us to the Grand Inquisitor in *The Brothers Karamazov*. In the novel, Ivan Karamazov tells a story in which Christ "decided to show Himself, if only for a moment, to His people, long-suffering, tormented, sinful people who loved Him with a child-like love."[5] People recognize him and are drawn to Him. But a cardinal of the church, the "Grand Inquisitor," realizes that the presence of Jesus is dangerous.[6] So he has Jesus arrested.

The ninety-year-old Grand Inquisitor says to Jesus, "You? Is it really you? . . . You need not answer me. Say nothing. I know only too well what you could tell me now. Besides, You have no right to add anything to what You said before. Did You come here to interfere and make things difficult for us?" The Grand Inquisitor then renders judgment on Jesus. He condemns Jesus for not fulfilling the people's needs—for not doing what the devil asked Jesus to do in the desert. The devil tried to offer the people bread, but Jesus "came empty-handed." The Grand Inquisitor tells Jesus, "You know that for the sake of that earthly bread, the spirit of the earth will rise up against You, will confront and conquer You, and they will all follow him shouting, 'Who is there to match the beast who has brought us fire from heaven?'"[7] In other words, the Grand Inquisitor is condemning Jesus for refusing to do—then and now—the miracles that make people happy. Jesus did not throw himself down from the temple, nor did he throw himself down from the cross. Instead, for the sake of obedience and the freedom to do God's will he endured the cross with its suffering and violence. Who wants that? It is not nice, and it certainly is not what the people seek.

Because the Grand Inquisitor wants the people to be happy, because he wants to meet the people's needs, and because he has grown weary of the ways of the Christian God, he tells Jesus: "We shall tell them that we are loyal to You and that we rule over them in Your name. We shall be lying, because we do not intend to allow You to come back."[8] For the sake of the people, this priest of the church recognizes that he must lie and do what Jesus refused to do—make the people happy by giving them the bread that Jesus refused to give. The Grand Inquisitor has lost his faith in that God. He no longer trusts a God who for the sake of freedom and obedience will tolerate suffering, judgment, and hell. The God found in Jesus simply cannot be trusted to meet people's perceived needs.[9] So the Grand Inquisitor creates a new god but doesn't change God's name. Now he controls this god's actions to insure that the people under his care will be protected from the living God.

Now put the Grand Inquisitor into a Mickey Mouse costume, make him sing "It's a small world after all," and we have the priests of our day who create the nice god, who teach us the prayer of Jabez, who remove the cross from the church.[10] We get the ecclesial authorities who tell us that god never makes judgments but is always there to accept us "with open hearts, open minds, open doors" (this is the name of a recent advertising campaign of the United Methodist Church). It is as if God has been reduced to a friendly character with open arms who meets us at the entrance to his magic kingdom, inviting us to come in and find our individual fulfillment.[11]

Of course, this god bears no relation to the God of Holy Scripture, but that may be a price we're willing to pay. For the Christian God seems to have let us down—all the violence, injustice, and oppression that has taken place in his name. The Christian God seems weak and ineffectual. When did he ever stop the torture of the innocent? Indeed, he even gives his own innocent Son over to torture and death!

Used as directed, the nice god promises results that are safe, effective, and enjoyable. The price appears small: we must live with the same lie as the Grand Inquisitor. But what is that compared to the cost of taking up a cross and following Christ? And our pain is less severe than the Grand Inquisitor's, for we anesthetize ourselves by continually denying that we have traded in the living God for a newer, nicer model. We continue to talk earnestly about worship and witness and service in Jesus' name. The nice god is the rope that binds, the gag that silences Jesus—but always in Jesus' name.

Where the Nice God Came From

There are two sources of the nice god—one cultural and the other theological. The nice god emerges from the therapeutic culture of late modernity where self-esteem and narcissism rule. The nice god who seeks only my spiritual fulfillment without the judgment of the cross and the wounds of Christ fits well a therapeutic culture intent on making persons whole who have no easily definable disease in the first place. But Christians might have resisted this god more powerfully if not for a fateful turn in theology around the time of the Reformation (the sixteenth century). That turn was the development of the idea that we cannot really know God, but can only know what God does "for us" or "in us." Together, these two historical changes transform God into a form of self-therapy for our perceived psychological needs.

Where does the therapeutic culture come from? Alasdair MacIntyre suggests that it begins with a loss of any socially or culturally agreed end or goal for human life.[12] Ends become matters of personal or group choice, not matters that are determined by our human nature or our social roles. To help us see the difference it makes, MacIntyre identifies three stock characters, three social roles that are characteristic of modernity. These three roles are the aesthete, the bureaucrat-manager, and the therapist. What they all have in common is that they assume there is no given end to human existence. Instead, each of these roles assumes that the task is to help social or individual bodies match means to ends where the ends can be whatever social or individual bodies themselves choose. Put more crudely, their job is to help people and institutions get what they want, because life comes without a specified purpose or goal.

Managers and therapists become experts at helping us achieve whatever end we choose for ourselves. They never make judgments about ends—what we should do—because such judgments would require the very agreement about the good life that we cannot reach. They concentrate on means—how to reach whatever goal has been chosen. So instead of developing moral wisdom about good ends, they develop technical expertise about good means—that is, efficient and effective means. Of course, if you look at the contemporary church, you can easily see how this technical expertise dominates the clergy.

In fact, a turn to expertise by the clergy has a long history. Perhaps it was the revivalist Charles Finney who first baldly stated this. Finney wrote that a revival is "not a miracle" where miracle is defined as "something above the powers of nature." Producing a revival "consists entirely in the right exercise of the powers of nature. It is just that and nothing else." Finney bluntly concludes: "It is a purely philosophical result of the right use of the constituted means—as much so as any other effect produced by the application of means."[13] Finney tells us a secret, similar to the one told us by the Grand Inquisitor. Conversions, revivals, and evangelical movements really have little or nothing to do with anything supernatural. They are simply the result of the application of appropriate social-scientific techniques. Just as the right marketing strategy can convince people to pay for water in a bottle (rather than drink it from the tap), so the right marketing strategy can convince people to pray for salvation. Revival is less a movement of the Spirit and more a mastery of the right means.

And what are the right means? Whatever will sell people a product they want or need, or convince them that they need this product for their own fulfillment. My own old-line liberal Protestant denomination, the United Methodist Church, recently launched a new advertising campaign to attract the "unchurched." This is the term church executives use to explain our target audience—disaffected persons between the ages of 25 and 54 who once attended church, but left because they found it too alienating, unwelcoming, and judgmental. We want to let them know that we have a church that welcomes them, accepts them as they are, and refuses to make judgments upon them. They will not be met at the door of our churches by some crucified Savior whose feet and hands bear the wounds of a rebellious creation. For the problem is not that they are sinners (that does not sell); the problem is that they are "unchurched." And why are they unchurched? Because people like me continue to say things like "we are all sinners who need to be forgiven by a risen crucified Savior." That doesn't sell; it is offensive. Thus the slogan for our commercial endeavor is "open hearts, open minds, open doors."[14] The people of the United Methodist Church are betting that there is a sufficient target audience of disaffected persons who think that the "traditional" church was exclusive, intolerant, judgmental, and incapable of meeting people's spiritual needs. (And the modern heresy of fundamentalism may have done sufficient damage that a number of such disaffected persons can be found.) I don't think that United Methodists are alone in thinking this.

But don't be fooled by all this talk of nonjudgmental evangelism. It is pious language that stands on the false assumption that the purpose of the Christian faith is to give our lives "meaning" and to satisfy our individual souls. The reason for the dominance of this language is understandable; it is the logical consequence of turning all Christians into potential

consumers and turning the church into nothing but a vendor
of goods and services—one more corporation vying in the
marketplace for its own special niche. Methodism, along with
lots of other denominations and congregations, has chosen
the niche of the nice god—the tolerant god who makes you
feel good.[15]

But this niche only appears tolerant. It actually uses the language of hospitality to cover a vindictive spirit. For what such
ads are truly saying is, "We are open and friendly unlike those
other churches that have hurt you; those churches that were
closed, exclusive, judgmental, and intolerant." What we are
really saying is, "Damn those churches that have hurt you and
caused you to be unchurched; we are not like them. We are a
nice, nonthreatening people, who serve a nice, nonthreatening
god who simply wants you to find your own spiritual fulfillment." And of course the "other side" says the same thing.
Conservative evangelical and liberal Protestant churches begin
to look the same. Both are vying for consumers in the religious
marketplace by selling an inoffensive deity who only "loves you
and has a wonderful plan for your life." And both claim the
other side is intolerant and judgmental. If I am right, then the
niceness we find dominating the contemporary church is just a
pretense, a hidden form of resentment that lets us position ourselves in the marketplace of churchgoers *against* all those forms
of churchgoing we despise and hold in contempt, especially all
those who came before us and did not understand our needs.
Far from being charitable, kind, or open to the Holy Spirit, the
sentimental niceness that characterizes much of the church
is a veiled form of power that allows us to hold the Christian
tradition in contempt and wage war against it, all the while
claiming to be its victim rather than its executioner. But this is
always done with a smile, a warm hug, and a happy face.

Thus, the nice god and the "friendly church" work hand-
in-hand to separate us from the judging, saving God revealed
in the cross of Christ.[16] The irony is that this wrong turn was
facilitated by the interest of Protestant theology in salvation.
Almost from the beginning, the primary focus of Protestant
reflection on Jesus was not on who he is, but on how he helps

us. Doctrinally, this makes Christology (the doctrine of who Christ is and what he does) a subset of soteriology (the doctrine of human salvation). A prime example of this is the claim by Philip Melanchthon that we cannot speak of Christ in himself, but can speak only of the benefits of Christ "for me."[17]

At first blush, this doesn't seem entirely objectionable. Being humble about our knowledge of God is a good thing, and Christians have focused on the saving significance of Jesus from the very beginning. Yet if the saving significance is the only thing we really know, then it is all too easily cut loose from Jesus to float away in the latest cultural breeze. We are left teetering on the point of this question: "Does he help me because he is the Son of God, or is he the Son of God because he helps me?" This danger becomes more obvious when we look at the thoroughly modern New Testament scholar, Rudolf Bultmann. When it comes to interpreting the claim that "Jesus is the Son of God," Bultmann suggests that this is not a statement "about the nature but only about the significance of Jesus."[18] In other words, to say that Jesus is divine is to say nothing at all about Jesus himself, but only to say something about his relationship to us—a relationship that is now freed of normative content. It is a small step from there to a nice salvation brought to you by a nice Jesus.

Of course, we might object to Bultmann's interpretation, but when we so emphasize Christ's benefits that he becomes nothing more than what his significance is "for me," we are in danger of repeating Bultmann's errors. Evangelism that says "come on, it's good for you"; discipleship that concentrates on the benefits package; sermons that "use" Jesus as the means to a better life or marriage or job or attitude—these all turn Jesus into an expression of that nice god who always meets my spiritual needs. And this is why I am increasingly hesitant to speak of Jesus as my *personal* Lord and Savior. As Ken Woodward put it in a 1994 essay, "Now I think we all need to be converted—over and over again, but having a personal savior has always struck me as, well, elitist, like having a personal tailor. I'm satisfied to have the same Lord and Savior as everyone else."[19] Jesus is not a personal Savior who only seeks to meet my needs. He is the risen crucified Lord of all creation who seeks to guide me back into the truth of the Triune God.

The Triune God: Serious Enough for Real Life

What if God is more concerned about goodness, truth, and holiness than our self-esteem or meeting our spiritual "needs" on our own terms? What if God is complete in himself and does not need us? That is God, according to traditional Christian teaching. Contemporary spiritual jargon has no capacity to recognize this moral and intellectual seriousness of the living God—a seriousness that ends on a cross and bears the wounds of a disordered creation. If there is any truth in what I have suggested—if the nice god of contemporary spirituality is a construction of ecclesiastical authority that seeks relevance to the dominant therapeutic culture, and if this god is constructed with the help of Protestantism's emphasis on the God "for us"—then it might be helpful to reflect on an earlier theological epoch, one before the dominance of the therapeutic culture over our spiritual language.

Two earlier times and earlier theologians will be of use for our reflection. They are helpful for, as Frederick Bauerschmidt has put it, these theologians lived on the "other edge of modernity." They lived before the rigid dogmas of a therapeutic culture settled over our everyday lives.[20] Although these two theologians are separated by a century, their work reveals the seriousness of the Triune God. First is Thomas Aquinas, the thirteenth-century theologian who taught us that God is the fullness of charity. Second is the fourteenth-century theologian Julian of Norwich, who taught us that God is kind.

For Thomas Aquinas, God does not need us. In fact, there is no "real relation" between God and creation because God has no "needs." That is to say God does not lack anything; God has no potentiality that must be fulfilled by something outside of himself. Instead God is "pure act." And that means God is without passion or change, for "passion" and "change" both imply that God passively receives something from outside of

God's self. God would receive something from us that God did not already have. We would supply God's "needs."

It is no surprise that in our modern therapeutic culture, when the nice god is constructed, Aquinas's teaching is objected to by all kinds of theologians. Modern theologians, like modern people, want a god with passion, a god who changes, a god who "needs" us in order to be complete. I fear that the reason for all this is because we want a god who will signify what we are, who will be like us. We cannot think God without first thinking of ourselves.

But for a theologian like Thomas Aquinas, it was still possible to think God without simply thinking ourselves, even though we could only use language from our sensible, everyday life to express these thoughts. God is Triune, three fully divine persons who are constituted by their relations to one another. Aquinas calls the Father, Son, and Holy Spirit "subsistent relations." Aquinas explains it this way: "As to essence, the Father is in the Son because the Father is his essence and he shares it with the Son without any change taking place in himself."[21] What does this mean? It means God is not like us, for we are not constituted entirely by our relations. No matter how much I seek to give myself to my wife, my children, my friends, I cannot give myself to them in the same way that the Triune Persons give themselves to each other. Nor do I exist because of that reciprocal giving and receiving. No matter how hard I try, I am not a "subsistent relation"—because I am not God.

Thus my relations are not complete in themselves; they always lack the kind of mutual self-giving that only the Triune God is. This lack causes suffering, change, and a dependence that must always be mediated through "words and actions which express only a partial giving of oneself even if one's intention is to give the whole of oneself."[22] But God can do more than partially give God's self. That is why we say the Triune God is defined by subsistent relations. And what does that mean "for us"? Not much, thanks be to God. It means that God does not need us for the sake of God's own self. God does not create because God is lonely. God does not create because God needs friends. God is not the lone patriarch, the strong silent type who secretly desires to "open up" to us but cannot do so without our help. God does not create because God has to. In fact, God's happiness, goodness, and truth are not dependent upon creation and its fate at all. One might be so bold as to say that if creation disappeared tomorrow, God would remain fully happy, good, and true because God is Triune, already complete and lacking nothing!

The doctrine of the Triune God is, therefore, much more morally and intellectually serious than the nice god who exists only to signify the satisfaction of our needs. God does not need us. God is not first and foremost for us. God is—as Triune—first and foremost for God's own self because only God in God's own self is truly good, charitable, and the fullness of life. God loves us because God loves God's self. This doesn't make God narcissistic, but it certainly does challenge the narcissism of our therapeutic culture. Creation and redemption do not satisfy some missing need in God's life. God creates because God loves his own goodness.[23] God is already the fullness of friendship, joy, and even conviviality. And without diminishing God's own fullness, we are invited to participate in that fullness. God seeks to share his life generously even though there is no compelling "need" to do so.[24] It is entirely gift.

So the Triune God may not be nice, when niceness implies that God's first task is to be "for us" in order to meet whatever spiritual needs we define. But this is not because God is unkind. It is because God loves as the Holy Trinity in a way we can never fully comprehend. God is true love—a love that knows no suffering—a love complete in itself. A love that gives itself away generously and invites us to participate in it—but a love that is so morally and intellectually serious that if you and I refuse to participate in it, God is not diminished. Who God is does not depend on God's significance for us.

For some reason, we moderns tend to think that our times, our suffering, and our concerns are so unique that we must fashion a god who can speak to them. We assume that older conceptions of God simply will not do "for us." It is interesting to compare this modern preoccupation with the thought of Julian of Norwich, who witnessed great suffering and yet found in the Triune God a source of comfort and strength. Listening to Julian of Norwich reveals that God is something far more profound than being nice; for Julian, God is kind precisely because God is Triune.

Julian received her revelations, or "showings," on what was thought to be her deathbed at the age of 30. She survived, eventually writing two versions of what she had seen.[25] What did God show Julian? She saw all creation as a ball the size of a hazelnut enfolded in the hand of God, and seeing this she realized that "it lasts and it ever shall last, for God loveth it. . . ."[26] Julian's revelation could wrongly be seen as an early version of the nice god. Her well-known statement, "all shall be well and all shall be well and all manner of thing shall be well" does sound something like a sentimental slogan on a Hallmark card. But Frederick Bauerschmidt has persuasively argued that we should not see Julian's work through the eyes of modern sentimentality.[27] After all, we have to remember that she wrote during the Black Death when one-third to one-half of Europe's population suffered or died. Yet even in the midst of some of the greatest suffering ever witnessed by human creatures, Julian saw God in terms of the trinitarian Christian faith. For Julian, unlike much of modern theology, God was not first and foremost power.[28] God was kind. She writes, "God is kind in his being."[29] Kindness here indicates "benevolence," the "nature" of a thing, and the relationship between things (think "kin" here). In all three of these meanings, God's nature is not pure power, but "kindness."[30] God's kindness to us is rooted in the kindness that is God's Triune life:

By the endless assent of the full accord of all the Trinity, the mid-person would be ground and head of this fair kind, out of whom we are all come, in whom we are all enclosed, into whom we shall all go; in him finding our full heaven in ever-lasting joy by the foreseeing purpose of all the blessed Trinity from without beginning; for before he made us he loves us; and when we were made we loved him; and this is a love made of the kindly substantial goodness of the Holy Ghost, mighty because of the might of the Father, and wise in mind of the wisdom of the Son; and thus is man's soul made by God and in the same point knit to God.[31]

We are knit to God by and through God's kindness, even though God is not knit to us.

For Julian, as Bauerschmidt notes, "humanity is eternally enfolded in God's love, because the creation of humankind is, through Christ, the eternal exemplar of creatures grounded in God's own Triune life. The love with which we love God is a participation in the 'kindly substantial goodness of the Holy Ghost,' the eternal love shared between the Father and the Son. And the revelation of this love in history is the cross."[32] And this helps make sense of her vision of the hazelnut. God's creation is as a "little thing, the quantity of a hazelnut in the palm of my hand that lasts and ever shall because God loves it."[33] Creation is enfolded within the Triune relations themselves. It is not "outside of" God, for there is no "outside of" God. As already mentioned, God is complete, the fullness of being. And yet creation isn't God. In other words, God respects the difference between God and creation by enfolding creation in God's own life. We see this especially in the incarnation, where the Creator becomes creature without ceasing to be Creator or destroying creation. Creation adds nothing to God, but while maintaining the distinction between God and creation, God becomes creation, joining it to God's self.

Why then does God create? Not because God needs to, or because God is always "for us" like some kind of personal talisman. God creates because God is love and God is kind and God is, in God's own self, gift and reception, the fullness of life. This kind God is the only kind of "god" that is worthy of our praise. The nice god isn't even a close second.

—— 3 ——

God Is
Not American

*Or, Why Christians Should Not Pledge Allegiance
to "One Nation under God"*

Michael J. Baxter

"I Always Thought Jesus Was an American"

"I know you're all going to think this is crazy, but I always thought Jesus was an American." This statement was uttered by a young woman in a seminar on the first century of Rome and the dawn of the Christian era at the University of California at San Diego. The seminar was taught by Mark Slouka, who reports the incident in an article entitled "A Year Later: Notes on America's Intimations of Mortality."[1] The main point of the article is that Americans think of themselves as separate from

55

the rest of the world, that they imagine themselves living in a strange physical and metaphysical isolation so that even after the attacks on the World Trade Center and the Pentagon, they have yet to come to grips with death. Americans only manage to absorb what Slouka calls (in a variation on the poem by Wordsworth) "intimations of mortality," subtle hints that history is not, as they often suppose, of their own making, under their own control. But such intimations are fleeting, he writes, passing quickly from the filth, the rotted flesh, and the smoldering bones of the world beyond American shores. Thus in the year following September 11, 2001, Americans dealt with the reality of death in their usual way: by denying it. "We erased it," Slouka observes, "carted it off in trucks. It had nothing to do with us. There was nothing to learn. We were still innocent, apart."[2]

What makes Americans so resilient in their denial of death? This is where Slouka's article is most insightful. It is, in a phrase, *American exceptionalism,* the myth of "America as an elect nation, the world-redeeming ark of Christ, chosen, above all the nations of the world, for a special dispensation."[3] It is this myth that the young woman articulated in the seminar that day. And this same myth, Slouka points out, has been articulated by a host of better-known articulators. It was initially articulated by John Winthrop, who in 1630 sermonized that the people sailing aboard the *Arbella* had been chosen for a special covenant with God to be "as a City upon a hill." Then there was Harriet Beecher Stowe, the nineteenth-century best-selling author, who in 1854 wrote that "the whole world has been looking towards America with hope, as a nation specially raised up by God to advance a cause of liberty and justice." And later, there were the evangelists of the Third Great Awakening, who envisioned an America "bounded to the north by Canada, to the south by Mexico, to the East by Eden, and to the West by the Millennium." And more recently, there was Ronald Reagan, who drew on Winthrop's city-on-a-hill image for his first inaugural address in 1981. Slouka argues that "although the specifically Christian foundation of American exceptionalism had been largely buried by the years, the self-conception built upon it—however secularized and given over to Mammon—remained intact."[4] America's national myth is, so to speak, still Christian after all these years.

An incident exhibiting the persistence of this Christian national myth arose in the summer of 2002, just in time for Slouka to be able to slip in a footnote reference to it. "Is all this talk of covenants and destiny merely a vestigial limb, a speechwriter's rhetorical trope?" he asks. "Hardly. We need only recall the recent reaction to the attempt by those godless liberals in the U.S. Court of Appeals to deprive us of our divine patrimony by excising the words 'under God' from the Pledge of Allegiance to understand the power of myth in America today."[5] The incident to which he refers had to do with the ruling from the Ninth Circuit Federal Court that the phrase "under God" in the Pledge is unconstitutional on grounds of the First Amendment's establishment clause in that it compels some citizens to acknowledge a reality contrary to their belief, namely God. The connection Slouka made is an appropriate one. Given the state of the national psyche after 9/11, this ruling touched a raw nerve, and in light of the hue and cry that rose up in its wake, it reminded us how widespread is the notion that the United States of America was founded on religious principles, that it is "one nation under God."

But this and similar expressions of America's national myth came into public prominence well before the Pledge of Allegiance controversy in the summer of 2002. Claims that the United States is a Christian nation could be seen and heard everywhere in the wake of 9/11, on billboards and business signs, on talk shows and TV programs, on email chains and Internet websites. One of the most controversial claims along these lines was that of Jerry Falwell, a leading spokesman for the so-called religious right who, in a discussion with Pat Robertson on the Christian Broadcast Network, suggested that the 9/11 attacks were a divine judgment visited upon this nation for what is being done by gays, lesbians, feminists, abortionists, the ACLU, the People for the American Way, and others who "have attempted to secularize America, have removed our nation from its relationship with Christ on which it was founded."[6] The problem with such statements is that they are so outlandish that many moderates, including moderate Christians, dismiss them as the talk of a few wacky religious fanatics from some backwater town in the Deep South who want to bring back the Scopes Monkey Trial. But the basic claim also comes from quarters that are far removed from the regions of religious fanaticism, though under the guise of more polished prose and sophisticated arguments.

"A Nation under God"

Take, for example, the editorial published in the December 2001 issue of *First Things,* a "mainstream" publication edited by Richard John Neuhaus. Entitled "In a Time of War," the editorial begins with a bald descriptive statement: "This is war. Call it a sustained battle or campaign, if you will, but the relevant moral term is war."[7] With the passion of one who witnessed the effects of September 11 firsthand, Neuhaus insists that "it is not, as some claim, a metaphorical war. Metaphorical airplanes flown by metaphorical hijackers did not crash into metaphorical buildings leaving thousands of metaphorical corpses. This is not virtual reality; this is reality. This is, for America and those who are on our side, a defensive war" (11).

The fact that Neuhaus and the neo-conservative crowd at *First Things* came out strongly in support of the invasion of Afghanistan is not very startling, given how the preponderance of commentators across a wide spectrum rushed to support this initial campaign in the war on terrorism. What is interesting, however, is Neuhaus's portrayal of the role of God in this war. This portrayal comes to the fore in his account of President Bush's televised speech to the nation on September 20, 2001. "In the coda of that historic speech," Neuhaus suggests, "boldness is touched by humility," and to illustrate he quotes from the president's speech itself: "The course of this conflict is not known, yet its outcome is certain. Freedom and fear, justice and cruelty have always been at war. And we know that God is not neutral between them. We will meet violence with patient justice, assured of the rightness of our cause and confident of the victories to come. In all that lies before us, may God grant us wisdom and may He watch over the United States of America" (11–12).

Neuhaus offers a defense of this part of Bush's speech in the next section of his editorial, with the subheading "A Nation Under God." He notes that some critics find in the president's words "not humility but hubris, an uncritical identification of our purposes with the purposes of God." To these critics, he delivers a blunt challenge:

> Let them make the case that between freedom and fear, between justice and cruelty, God *is* neutral. Let them make the case that those who have declared war against us do *not* intend to instill fear by inflicting cruelty. Assured as we are and must be of the rightness of our cause, the President submits that cause in prayer to a higher authority. In a time of grave testing, America has once again given public expression to the belief that we are "one nation under God"—meaning that we are under both His protection and His judgment. This is not national hubris. Confidence that we are under his protection is faith; awareness that we are under His judgment is humility. This relationship with God is not established by virtue of our being Americans, but by the fact that He is the Father of the common humanity of which we are part. Most Americans are Christians who understand the mercy and justice of God as revealed in the gospel of Jesus Christ. Recognizing the danger that the motto "For God and country" can express an idolatrous identity of allegiances, most Americans act in the hope that it represents a convergence of duties. All Americans, whatever their ultimate beliefs, have reason to hope that reality is not neutral in this war against the evil of terrorism. (12)

Neuhaus's argument here is problematic in several respects. For one thing, it casts the war on terrorism in the exaggerated terms of a struggle for freedom and justice against cruelty and fear, and thus fails to acknowledge the possibility that neither the United States nor al-Qaeda may be on the side of freedom and justice (properly understood) or that both may be given to spreading cruelty and fear. Possibilities such as these do not appear when the world is viewed through the simplistic lens of Neuhaus (and Bush). For another thing, after identifying the cause of the United States with the cause of freedom and justice, it employs a flawed argument to align both of these causes to the purposes of God. The argument is flawed because, while it is true, as Neuhaus argues, that God is not neutral when it comes to freedom and justice, it is also true that God's purposes may well be aligned with a form of freedom and justice that is represented neither by the United States nor by al-Qaeda, but rather by some other political entity or body or by the church itself.

And then, beyond these two problems, there is the more far-reaching problem of the vague, unspecified identity of the deity to which Neuhaus refers when he states that "America has once again given public expression to the belief that we are 'one nation under God.'" This vagueness is reflected in his wizened concept of faith as "confidence that we are under His protection," which falls far short of a more traditional definition of faith as the virtue or habit whereby the person gives intellectual assent to revealed truths regarding the identity and nature of God, including, for example, the truths about the Trinity.[8] This vagueness is also evident in his truncated definition of humility as "awareness that we are under His judgment," which is true, but which must also be defined as the virtue whereby the person is restrained in his pursuit of great goods by subjecting himself to God, for whose sake he also humbles himself to others.[9] Now both faith and humility are understood in Christian tradition to be theological or infused virtues—that is, virtues given by grace—and as such they cannot be realized apart from life in Christ and in the church. Therefore any definition of faith and humility must include an account of the concrete practices, specific virtues, and forms of life entailed in being Christian.

But Neuhaus fails to include such an account, probably because this would render his argument too ecclesially specific to qualify as public discourse in a pluralistic setting such as the United States. So, instead, he ventures the claim that "most Americans are Christians who understand the mercy and justice of God as revealed in the gospel of Jesus Christ" (12). This is a deeply questionable claim, but useful for Neuhaus. It fortifies his notion of a "convergence of duties" to God and country while never acknowledging that Americans worship strikingly different gods, whether it be the god of New Age crystal users in Seattle, Buddhists in the Bay Area, Black Bumper Mennonites in Ohio, Mormons in Utah, and so on. As for those who do not believe in God at all, Neuhaus provides the assurance that "reality is not neutral in this war on terrorism" either, thereby offering a variation on the for-God-and-country theme: for reality and country (12). In either case, Americans can rest assured that as their nation goes to war, it does so under this all-purpose higher power that Neuhaus calls "God." All of which is to say that the god Neuhaus invokes is the god of American civil religion, a god of and for the United States.

Christians as "Alien Citizens"

Neuhaus commends the upsurge of patriotism following September 11, but he also attempts to clarify his position by drawing a distinction between rendering to God and rendering to Caesar (see Mark 12:13–17). Admitting that Jesus' reply to the Pharisees posits a distinction that Christians "will probably never get just exactly right," Neuhaus notes that nevertheless "it is agreed by all that the emphasis falls on the second injunction—do not render to Caesar what is God's. Whether with respect to patriotism, wealth, family, or anything else, it is always a matter of the right ordering of our loves and loyalties" (12).

To elaborate on this point, Neuhaus directs our attention to the *Letter to Diognetus*, a second-century, anonymously authored text, from which he offers the following quotation (the asterisks are explained below):

Christians are not distinguished from the rest of humanity by either country, speech, or customs. They do not live in cities of their own; they use no peculiar language, they do not follow an eccentric manner of life.* They reside in their own countries, but only as alien citizens, and endure everything as foreigners. Every foreign country is their homeland, and every homeland a foreign country.** They obey the established laws, but in their own lives they go beyond the law.*** In a word: what the soul is in the body, that Christians are in the world. The soul dwells in the body, but does not belong to the body; just so Christians live in the world, but are not of the world. (12)

According to Neuhaus, this passage shows that "these 'alien citizens,' still far from their true home in the New Jerusalem that is history's consummation, have followed the course of Christian fidelity in accepting responsibility for the well-being of what is their home in time before the End Time." In other words, Christians have an ultimate love and loyalty toward God, yet a penultimate love and loyalty to their homeland; they have an ordered love both for God and country.

What is noteworthy, and troubling, about this quotation is that in several instances it deletes significant portions with no acknowledgement of having done so, not even ellipses. In this important and admittedly delicate matter, only a display of the deleted portions of the text will suffice. There are three such deletions from the original text, each of which I want to present and then comment on.

The first deleted section (noted above by the single asterisk) reads as follows:

Their teaching is not the kind of thing that could be discovered by the wisdom or reflection of mere active-minded men; indeed, they are not outstanding in human learning as others are. Whether fortune has given them a home in a Greek or foreign city, they follow local custom in the matter of dress, food, and way of life; yet the character of the culture they reveal is marvelous and, it must be admitted, unusual.[10]

In this passage, Christian teaching is described as distinct from conventional wisdom and as not based on outstanding human learning. And Christians themselves are portrayed as both similar and different—similar in respect to their dress, food, and way of life; different in respect to "the culture they reveal," which is described as "marvelous" and "unusual." It is not clear what their being simultaneously similar and different means concretely in this passage, but some hints can be found in the two other deleted passages.

The second deleted passage (see the double asterisk) reads this way:

> They marry like the rest of men and beget children, but they do not abandon their babies that are born. They share a common board, but not a common bed. In the flesh as they are, they do not live according to the flesh. They dwell on earth, but are citizens of heaven.[11]

Here we see that Christians, unlike others of their day, do not "abandon," that is to say, abort their children (or as another translation has it, they do not commit infanticide by exposing their children). And while they share a common board, they do not share a "common bed" (or as it is put in another translation, "they share their meals, but not their wives"). Avoiding these practices is seen as part of "not liv[ing] according to the flesh," as part of their being "citizens of heaven." Thus Christians do not accommodate themselves to the country they live in; they are different from others in important ways, such as the way they marry and have children.

In other words, there is a sharp and costly tension between Christians and others, as can be seen in the third deleted passage (see the triple asterisk):

> They love all men, but are persecuted by all. They are unknown, and yet they are condemned. They are put to death, yet are more alive than ever. They are paupers, but they make many rich. They lack all things, and yet in all things they abound. They are dishonored, yet glory in their dishonor. They are ma-

ligned, and yet are vindicated. They are reviled, and yet they bless. They suffer insult, yet they pay respect. They do good, yet are punished with the wicked. When they are punished, they rejoice, as though they were getting more of life. They are attacked by the Jews as Gentiles and are persecuted by the Greeks, yet those who hate them can give no reason for their hatred.[12]

In this passage, the identity of Christians as "alien citizens" involves being condemned, put to death, impoverished, dishonored, maligned, reviled, insulted, punished, attacked, and persecuted. This is not their fault, the author makes clear, using a rhetorical pattern taken from the apostle Paul (2 Cor. 4:12; 6:9–10). Though mistreatment is often their lot, they respond to persecution by loving, enriching, blessing, and paying respect to others.

Each of these three passages quoted above, then, reveals that for the second-century author of the *Letter to Diognetus*, Christians are significantly different from others in both their beliefs and their practices. So much are Christians different that they are often at odds with people around them to the point of being regularly hated and sometimes killed. But when Neuhaus omits these passages, a strikingly different impression is created, the impression that ancient Christian teaching calls for the kind of love of God and country that is commended in his editorial. And this impression is put to the service of Neuhaus's more specific message that love of God and country is especially fitting for Christians in the United States because it is "a nation under God," or "an overwhelmingly Christian nation rooted, albeit sometimes tenuously, in the Judeo-Christian moral tradition."

The Story of "Christian America"

This notion of a "Christian America" is usually presented in the form of a story of how the nation was founded. More often than not, the story features the role played by members of a particular denomination, usually the same denomination as the one telling the story. When Congregationalists tell the story of America's founding, for example, the setting is in Massachusetts and the main characters come over on the Mayflower. When Baptists tell the story, the action occurs in Rhode Island with Roger Williams playing the lead role. Methodists tend to emphasize the Second Great Awakening in the formation of the nation. As for Catholics, they underscore the contribution of the colony of Maryland in the U.S. founding. Thus each Christian denomination tells the story of the founding of the nation with its own unique setting and characters, but they all make the same basic point that America is a Christian nation.

Neuhaus's story of America is of this vintage, but with a peculiar twist, reflecting his own journey from Lutheranism to Roman Catholicism. His story goes like this: Once upon a time in America, British colonists banded together to throw off the tyrannical rule of their king and founded a form of government designed to protect the rights of its citizens with respect to freedom of speech, assembly, the press, and religion. This last freedom listed was in fact "the first freedom," the most important one, for it prohibited the establishment of any one particular religion as the official religion of the land and instead guaranteed the free exercise of religion for all. This warded off the possibility that the nation would plunge itself into a New-World version of Europe's "wars of religion" while at the same time ensuring that its public life would be guided by the moral and intellectual principles to which its Christian citizens (or the vast majority of them at any rate) subscribed. Throughout the nineteenth and into the twentieth century, this ingenious combination of "ordered liberty," unprecedented in world history, proved to be a formula that brought the nation through the crisis of civil war, enabled it to welcome waves of European and other immigrants to its shores, and allowed it to afford greater measures of freedom to its citizens, particularly women and African Americans. It also provided the nation with the fortitude needed to fight political tyranny abroad in the First World War, the Second

World War, and the subsequent Cold War, all of which were waged on the strength of the so-called Judeo-Christian tradition, a moral and intellectual consensus that now included greater numbers of Catholics, Jews, and (some) secularists.

But at some point in this more recent phase of the nation's history, another moral and intellectual perspective emerged, one that regarded any public profession of religious belief or a religion-based morality as constituting a threat to the rights of individuals whose religious or moral beliefs stand outside this supposed nationwide consensus. The emergence of this new perspective can be traced back to any number of cultural trends earlier in the twentieth century, but it gained political and cultural ascendancy in the 1960s, when it became anathema to invoke religious and moral principles in public discourse. This constituted a threat to the very foundations on which the nation was founded. The main culprits were left-leaning politicians, journalists, intellectuals, church leaders, and other members of the so-called cultural elite, who also have been derisively labeled "Bobos in paradise" (in a recent book that Neuhaus has touted[13])—that is, baby-boomers who sported a bohemian lifestyle and radical politics when coming of age in the 1960s and then, in the ensuing decades, made their way into the higher echelons of U.S. society where they exercise an alarming degree of influence over the central institutions of the nation: the government, the press, universities, and the mainstream churches. This created what Neuhaus called "the naked public square," and in a book under this title published in 1984 he called for a re-infusion of religious and moral principles into American public discourse, a re-clothing, so to speak, of this naked public square.[14] This re-clothing became possible during the 1980s, first through the resurgence of conservative-minded evangelical Christians and then of Catholics. Neuhaus called the latter "the Catholic moment."[15]

In light of this storyline, the significance of Neuhaus's claim that America is a Christian nation comes into fuller view. It simultaneously does two things. First, it harks back to the founding of the nation and decries the recent betrayal of that founding by those who deny the nation's religious and moral roots. Second, it calls for a religious and moral renewal of America that rescues the nation from its present malaise, a renewal to be led by the Catholics. Witness a twelve-part series of columns in *First Things* on the idea of "Christian America," the last of which came out in May 2001 coyly titled "Something Like, Just Maybe, A Catholic Moment."[16]

"An Overwhelmingly Christian Nation"?

How accurate is Neuhaus's post-9/11 claim that America is "rooted, albeit sometimes tenuously, in the Judeo-Christian moral tradition"? The statement's subordinate clause—"albeit sometimes tenuously"—acknowledges that the nation's Judeo-Christian tradition at times has been obscured or attacked. But this caveat is clearly outweighed by the overriding claim that America is "overwhelmingly Christian." As a way of backing up this claim, Neuhaus notes "that following the [September 11] attack, the first gathering of national leadership and the first extended, and eloquent, address by the President was in a cathedral. And that Irving Berlin's 'God Bless America' is getting equal time, at least, with the less religiously explicit national anthem. And that children in public schools gather in the classroom for prayer. And that the fallen beams of the World Trade Center, forming a cross, are blessed as the semi-official memorial to the victims. Intellectuals are forever in search of 'the real America.' The weeks following the attack of September 11 provided one answer to that search. It is an America that Tocqueville would recognize, even if it surprised, and no doubt offended, many intellectuals" (15).

The claims Neuhaus makes here are again problematic on several scores. First, he cites the national prayer service and prayers being said in schools as evidence that the United States is a Christian nation. But the national prayer service, although it was held in a cathedral, included prayers recited by a Jewish rabbi and a Muslim imam. Would *they* agree that they live in a Christian nation? And would this be the view of Irving Berlin, the Jewish composer of "God Bless America"? And is it really true that the fallen beams arranged in the form of a cross made fitting, semi-official memorial for those who died? Including those who were Jewish? or Hindu? or atheist?

Moreover, Neuhaus suggests that the America that emerged in the weeks after the attacks is "an America that Tocqueville would recognize," but what he does not mention is that the "god" that emerged during those weeks is likewise one that Tocqueville would recognize.[17] This is because Tocqueville's god, as scholars of his work have pointed out, is a peculiarly modern god, one that serves to keep society and the state intact in this disenchanted, post-Christian world. It is thus a different god from the God who is named and praised in traditional Christian belief and practice.[18] In Neuhaus's enthusiasm for "the new patriotism," which he judges to be "all in all, a very good thing," he does not address the contested aspects of Tocqueville's "America" and "god."

But the most obvious problem in Neuhaus's claim that America is a Christian nation is that it does not account for the fact that Americans in large numbers engage in practices that run clearly counter to the Christian way of life, practices related to marrying and having children, to cite the two that are emphasized in the *Letter to Diognetus*. If America is a Christian nation, what are we to make of the fact that roughly 50 percent of all marriages in America end in divorce? Further, if America is a Christian nation, what are we to do with the fact that each year in America there occur more than one million abortions?

In spite of all this, Neuhaus clearly thinks that it is a Christian nation. But if challenged on this point, his argument does not refer us to America in the present, but rather to an America of the past and of the future—of a glorious past, when America was founded and developed as a Christian nation, and of a promising future, when America will reclaim its legacy and return to its founding religious and moral principles. When it comes to the present, his argument only refers us to the struggle to bring the nation out of its current crisis and calls us to join traditional Christians and other religiously and morally conservative Americans in this struggle.

And a monumental struggle it is, for in the final section of the editorial, we learn that America is engaged in a "war of centuries," indeed "a war of religion." This is not to say that America wishes to engage in such a war. "We of the West," Neuhaus assures us, "definitively put wars of religion behind us with the Treaty of Westphalia in 1648. But that was a piece of the story of the West of which Islam was not part and for which Islam has no counterpart" (16). As a result, a war of religion has been thrust upon America by the adherents of Islam who have stored up for decades, if not centuries, a burning hatred for the West and who have not integrated into their worldview the values of Western democracy. To those who insist that Americans should embrace the otherness of Islam in the name of diversity, Neuhaus gives this rejoinder: "With respect to freedom, human rights, and the dignity of the person, their difference is not a diversity to be celebrated but a threat to be opposed. The terrorists have now unmistakably underscored their otherness, and with it the otherness of Islam" (16). To those who insist that Islam is not antithetical to democratic values, he declares that it is up to Muslims to demonstrate this themselves. For the time being, however, what the 9/11 attacks indicate is that, as he puts it with remarkable bluntness: "They are other" (16). Not mentioning that Christ died for these others, he goes on to cite an article by Bernard Lewis in the *Atlantic* that underscores what is at stake in this two-sided struggle. "When Muslims speak of the West," he explains,

> they mean the Christian West. They mean Christendom. Many in the West want to believe that ours is a secularized culture, but Lewis reminds us that most Muslims view secularization itself as a form of specifically Christian decadence. Today many in the West are asking, Who are they? We cannot ask Who are they? without also asking Who are we? More and more, as this war continues, we may come to recognize that we are, however ambiguously, who they think we are, namely, the Christian West. (16)

As Neuhaus tells the story, America has now been drawn into a monumental struggle between Islam and the Christian West, a struggle that is spurring Americans to reclaim their identity as citizens of a Christian nation. In this sense, the post–September 11 display of patriotism can be taken as a hopeful development. The flags, the patriotic songs on the radio, the teachers and students praying at school, the upsurge in church attendance—all these are signs of America undergoing its restoration as a Christian nation.

What is ironic about this depiction of the nation is that in the fall of 1996 Neuhaus & Company were raising fundamental questions about the tenuous state of American democracy—calling America a "regime" and "the tyrant state"—and even suggesting the need for civil disobedience. Yet in the fall of 2001 democracy in America is the beacon of freedom, human rights, and human dignity for the rest of the world. How are we to explain this remarkable shift in thematics? Surely it has something to do with the election of President Bush in the intervening years, which, in the worldview of the neo-conservatives, buoyed the condition of the nation. But this points to a deeper reason that strikes closer to the heart of the issue. The reason is that Neuhaus has linked the destiny of Christianity to the future of liberal democratic nations in the Christian West, in particular to the future of what he considers to be the leader among these nations, the United States of America. As a result, the struggle to reclaim America as a Christian nation gets transmuted into a struggle over the terrestrial future of Christianity itself, a struggle of almost ultimate significance. In this context, reservations about America quickly move into the background for the sake of prevailing in the broader struggle for the survival of America and the Christian West.

To be fair, we should note that Neuhaus reminds us that Christians place their ultimate loyalty in no earthly city but in the city that is their final destination, the heavenly Jerusalem—an eschatological proviso, so to speak, meant to safeguard against an idolatrous allegiance to country. But no safeguard is effective without an accompanying *ecclesiological* proviso, without a positive and substantive account of the church.[19]

Interestingly, there is no such account in Neuhaus's editorial. There are plenty of references to God, to Christians, to the Judeo-Christian tradition, to America as a Christian nation, but no clear references to the church. This is not surprising, of course, for to focus on ecclesiology would bring up a host of theological issues over which Christians in the United States have deep differences. It could generate division when what is needed in a time of national crisis, "in a time of war," is unity. Neuhaus would object to this characterization, of course, by pointing out that time and again he has not hesitated to tackle important ecclesiological issues in *First Things* and in his other published writings. Nevertheless, he does not do so when it comes to the nation going to war. This is because he conceives of political community in terms of the politics of nation-states, one nation-state in particular, the United States. In doing so, his terms must be tailored to the exigencies of a religiously pluralistic society, the primary exigency being that ecclesially specific terms must be separated from politics. As a result, when he moves into the political sphere to take up political issues such as going to war, his references to God are cast in the general terms of civil theology, such as "religion, "Christianity," and the "Judeo-Christian tradition." In spite of his insistence that America is "under God," any and all reference to the church—that is, the community of those baptized in the name of the Father and of the Son and of the Holy Spirit—recedes into the background.

On this score, it is no wonder that Neuhaus favors the description in the *Letter to Diognetus* of the church as the soul of the world. As he quotes it, the passage reads: "In a word: what the soul is in the body, that Christians are in the world. The soul dwells in the body, but does not belong to the body; just so Christians live in the world, but are not of the world" (12). The impression created with this quotation is that the relation between body and soul is peaceful and harmonious. Just as the soul is an incorporeal reality that gives unity and coherence to the body, so the church is an incorporeal reality that gives unity and coherence to the world. But here again, Neuhaus's citation of the *Letter to Diognetus* is misleading, for as we read on in the text itself, we learn that the relationship between body and soul is neither peaceful nor harmonious. From where the quotation leaves off, the *Letter* continues by drawing a parallel between the conflict of the soul and the flesh and the conflict between Christians and the world. The *Letter* reads:

> The flesh hates the soul and acts like an unjust aggressor, because it is forbidden to indulge in pleasures. The world hates Christians—not that they have done it wrong, but because they oppose its pleasures. The soul loves the body and its members in spite of the hatred. So Christians love those who hate them. The soul is locked up in the body, yet it holds the body together. And so Christians are held in the world as in a prison, yet it is they who hold the world together. The immortal soul dwells in a mortal tabernacle. So Christians sojourn among perishable things, but their souls are set on immortality in heaven. When the soul is ill-treated in the matter of food and drink, it is improved. So, when Christians are persecuted, their numbers daily increase. Such is the assignment to which God has called them, and they have no right to shirk from it.[20]

This passage depicts Christians, as often as not, coming into conflict with the world, with whatever "city" they reside in. As the soul orders the unruly, pleasure-seeking passions of the body by revealing to it the love that emanates from God, so Christians order the unruly, pleasure-seeking cities of the world by revealing to them the peace that likewise emanates from God.

On this (properly contextualized) reading of the *Letter to Diognetus,* the church is the one community in which the obligations of Christians to the cities of this world are properly ordered to the love of God. For this reason, the cities of this world are never "under God" in such a way that Christians may pledge their allegiance to them. Such an allegiance is proper only to Christ and the church. Indeed, in view of the entire *Letter to Diognetus,* it becomes apparent that the primary concern of its second-century author is to enjoin Christians to avoid worshiping the false gods of the world's cities, gods whose patronage is presented in the city's myths as essential to their security and flourishing. But this is always accomplished by shedding blood, the blood of those who protect the city from its enemies. Beyond the danger of worshiping the gods of various cities, there was also the danger of worshiping the gods of Rome, a particular concern in the *Letter to Diognetus*. These gods plausibly promised a peace that would reign throughout the entire empire, the *Pax Romana,* and yet, like the many forms of civil peace in the ancient world, it was a "peace" founded on imperial violence and was, as the Christians saw it, not true peace at all, not the peace of Christ.

One *Church* under God

All this talk of Christians worshiping the false gods of ancient cities and empires would seem quaint were it not for the fact that this danger has its modern counterparts. In modernity, of course, the many "cities" have been replaced by nations, and Christians find themselves very much at home in them. Indeed, a disturbingly familiar feature of Christianity in modernity is that the churches have divided into national churches with Christians fighting other Christians on behalf of their particular nation. During World War I, Christians in Germany and Austria fought against Christians in France, England, and the United States. The same was true during World War II and numerous other wars besides: the war over the Falkland Islands, the war in the former Yugoslavia, the war in Kosovo, the two wars with Iraq (inasmuch as Iraq is the home for about 1,000,000 Christians).

This early phase in the war on terrorism is different, according to Neuhaus and others, because it is not a war among Christians but between Islam and the Christian West. But this war is sure to expand as the United States pursues a foreign policy that, like that of ancient Rome, promises a new comprehensive peace for all the nations of the world, a *Pax Americana.* And as it does expand, Christians—those in the United States and those who are scattered in rather large numbers throughout the Middle East—will again face the temptation of pledging their allegiance to their nation. But Christians in the United States face the most challenging temptation, for they live in an *imperium* that itself claims to be Christian. This makes it more difficult to resist the ideology embedded in the notion "one nation under God," and all the more urgent to develop an ecclesiology centering on the principle of "one *church* under God."

Developing such an ecclesiology could take as its starting point the image in the *Letter to Diognetus* of the church as a soul that gives the world a unity that it would otherwise not have, thus overcoming the division of the body of the world into nations and empires. But this body/soul analogy brings with it some serious shortcomings, as analogies always do. For if the church is a soul, then it must be invisible, whereas in fact the church is visible; indeed, it is itself a body with Christ as the head and Christians as the members (see Col. 1:18; 1 Cor. 12:12–31; Rom. 12:4–6). The church is more appropriately understood as a body whose members are united to Christ and each other through the invisible power of the Holy Spirit but whose communal life is marked by a charity that is visible, embodied. This is why the apostle Paul describes baptism as being engrafted into Christ's body. This is also why he emphasized the intrinsic relation between the Lord's Supper and the unity that is a mark of the Christian community (1 Cor. 11:17–34). United as such, the members of the church are able to offer their bodies as a living sacrifice, dedicated and acceptable to God (Rom. 12:1–3). The image here is of the priesthood of the Levites, the tribe designated by God to make animal or cereal offerings for the sake of the reconciliation of all Israel; but now Christians unite themselves with the offering of the Son to the Father, so that through the power of the Holy Spirit they become "a chosen race, a royal priesthood, a holy nation, God's own people" (1 Peter 2:9). Here too, it is important to notice how this imagery indicates that the church extends the mission of Israel. While no longer defined by its claims on the land and on its physical descent from Abraham, the church is nevertheless the community that has fallen heir to the gift and the call of Israel. Hence the appellation that appears toward the end of Paul's Letter to the Galatians: "the Israel of God" (Gal. 6:16).

The importance of bestowing the name "Israel" on the church is that it precludes any use of that name in reference to a nation, as in the national *mythos* where America is understood as "the New Israel." In so doing, it also rejects the idea that a nation-state is peculiarly "a nation under God." Rather the church itself, like Israel in the Bible, is a nation, that is, a people with a common history and destiny, identity and mission; and yet at the same time, the church is, again like Israel, set apart as a light to the nations. In a time of war, therefore, the challenge of Christians, scattered among the nations of the world, is to live as the one body of Christ and to pledge their allegiance not to one nation under God, but to one church under God.

— 4 —

God Is
Not
a Capitalist

Michael L. Budde

In a June 18, 1998, news story, dateline Vatican City but with ecumenical significance, the following was reported:

> *In a historic reversal of its nearly 2000-year-old pro-meek stance, the Catholic Church announced Tuesday that it is permanently rescinding the traditional "blessed" status of the world's meek. "Our Lord and Savior Jesus Christ once said, 'Blessed are the meek,'" said Pope John Paul II in a papal bull read before the College of Cardinals. "However, there has always been a tacit understanding between the Church and the meek that this 'blessed' status was conditional upon their inheritance of the earth, an event which seems unlikely to happen anytime in the foreseeable future. Our relationship, therefore,*

must be terminated." . . . Citing "two millennia of inaction and
non-achievement" by the world's impoverished and downtrodden,
the pope contended that the meek's historic inability to improve their
worldly status constituted "bad faith" on their part.

"Twenty centuries should have been more than enough time
for them to inherit the earth," the Supreme Pontiff said. "For
years, the Catholic Church has made every effort to help them,
but at some point, enough is enough. We are patient, but we
are not saints."

[Other high churchmen offered interpretations of the Pope's
decision.] "Everything about the meek, from their simple gar-
ments to their quiet demeanors to their utter lack of can-do
spirit, goes against Church philosophy," Cardinal Jean-Claude
Turcotte of Montreal said. "Sitting back and expecting the Lord
to provide is not the type of behavior for which the Church
should be rewarding its followers."

The article continued: *In an effort to move away from its tradi-*
tional meek core demographic and attract more upscale worshipers,
Vatican officials announced a number of changes for the Gospels.
Among them: Christ shall be said to have been born in a rustic-but-
spacious birthing suite and not a manger, with the amount of gold
and frankincense bestowed upon Him by the wise men quadrupled
and the amount of myrrh halved; it shall henceforth be as easy for
a rich man to enter Heaven as it is for a camel to pass through a
heated three-car garage; and the episode between Christ and the
moneylenders in the temple shall from now on be interpreted as
an internecine argument over appropriately aggressive fundraising
tactics."

Concluded the Pope: "Screw the meek."[1]

Not the *New York Times* or the *Chicago Tribune* or the
Associated Press—this dramatic news story appeared in a Madison, Wisconsin, paper called *The Onion*. This journal's forte is
fictitious news stories intended to make a point about societal
absurdities, hypocrisy, and arrogance. Obviously you didn't
miss an official pronouncement about a revised Sermon on the
Mount. The point of this fairly audacious satire, offered with
the subtlety of a sledgehammer, is that church attitudes toward
commerce and the market de facto trump its scriptural mandate
to privilege the poor, the outcast, and the oppressed. Were we

honest about matters, the folks at *The Onion* imply, we would rewrite the Gospels to accord with our true beliefs, convictions, and practices. "Screw the meek," in other words.

That we would even consider the negation "God is not a capitalist" says volumes about how deeply capitalist logic has penetrated the assumptions and practices of Christians—Protestant, Catholic, and Orthodox alike. We are not, after all, seeking to disprove a patently absurd thesis, like "God is an organ grinder's monkey." Yet I hope to show how the claim that God is a capitalist is almost as absurd as the claim that God is an organ grinder's monkey.

All of this is more than idle exercise of theological speculation, for whatever we conclude God is or is not should have an important influence on what we think the church should or should not be. If God is merciful, the church should not be vengeful; if God is not a white supremacist, neither should God's church be a white supremacist institution. It is with this relationship between our theology of God and our theology of church—our ecclesiology—that I want to begin our exploration. In fact, I want to work backward through the relationship. For while there are relatively few people brazen enough to suggest that God is a capitalist, there are countless numbers of people, including church leaders, who assert that the church should be more like a modern, for-profit corporation. If that is an appropriate ecclesiology (doctrine of the church)—if the church should be more like Microsoft or Disney or ServiceMaster (and not, of course, like Enron or Arthur Andersen)—then the Lord we serve must be the Chief Executive Officer, the Chairman of the Board, the Divine Entrepreneur. If we hold that humanity is made in the image and likeness of God (Gen. 1:27), and if we believe that human nature essentially is capitalist, then God may, in fact, be a capitalist.

The Church as Corporation

Churches have always derived some sense of organization, of administration, of the practice of their common life, from surrounding nonreligious institutions. From the Catholic adoption of the diocesan model of the Roman Empire to the Protestant introduction of representative democracy into church governance, Protestant and Catholic church practices have always experienced patterns of mutual interaction with their environment. In our day, however, there is a vigorous movement toward making churches more like for-profit corporations as the solution to a variety of ecclesial weaknesses—to compensate for clergy shortages, to utilize more effectively modern approaches to communications, fund-raising, and financial management, to carry out the mandate of the Great Commission more efficiently, and much more. This trend expresses something I call "Christianity Incorporated"—a mutual exchange between churches and for-profit corporations in which they imitate and mimic one another in some new and potentially disconcerting ways.[2]

Allow me to provide a few examples of what I mean. We live in a cultural ecology in which people are exposed to a steady flood of commercial messages, prompts, jingles, logos, and other forms of advertising, marketing, and public relations—as many as 16,000 per day according to some studies. Increasingly, mainline Protestant and Catholic churches have come to join their evangelical brethren in embracing the strategies, tactics, and ideology of Madison Avenue. As a result, we get developments like the following.

Like the Rolling Stones and other major concert acts, the Catholic Church has now taken on corporate sponsorship to underwrite the world tours of its major performer, Pope John Paul II. To finance his 1998 visit to Mexico City, the Archdiocese of Mexico City entered into sponsorship arrangements with more than two dozen firms, most of them major multinationals. The single largest sponsor, the Pepsi Cola-owned Sabritas chip company, paid $1.8 million for the right to use the pope's image in its advertising and packaging. The company's Spanish-language play on words—"Las Papas del Papa" (the potatoes of the pope)—was lost on absolutely no one; nor were the slogans and appeals of the other companies who plastered the pope's image on billboards, print ads, and other locations in association with firms including a local cement company, Mercedes-Benz, American Express, and the local Bimbo bread company.

In the United Kingdom, the five major Christian groups (including the Church of England and the Catholic Church) have backed major advertising campaigns aimed at boosting church attendance and the public image of the churches. Using the tools of the for-profit culture industries (e.g., television, advertising, movies, marketing) also requires adopting the ideological assumptions of those industries, including "don't get people depressed." This group of churches sponsored an advertising campaign to boost Easter church attendance that deliberately omitted any references to the cross, lest such a "downer" symbol affect the positive response rate of the campaign. On other occasions the Church of England has attempted to reposition itself by sponsoring advertising campaigns built around wealthy and attractive models and celebrities, hip music scores, and lavish production qualities. Luxury car makers, clothing designers, and other corporations have been most eager to place their products in church commercials because, to them, the religion market remains underexploited terrain.

The Anglican Church's director of communications now openly refers to church members not as Christians but as "customers." As he says, "if we are going to make a contribution to the nation the Church has to be more businesslike."[3] While another spokesperson admits that "there will be people who say we are prostituting ourselves by trying to sell the Church," such is necessary because "we want to move away from the 'churchy' image of stained-glass windows and old ladies in hats."[4] Once one moves from congregants to customers, the logic is relentless and its effects on church life not easily contained. One Anglican bishop has urged churches to rearrange worship times in order to avoid conflict with popular football matches,[5] while the former Archbishop of Canterbury George Carey wants liturgies aimed at keeping customers happy and on schedule. As he says, "I have a theory that more people would come to church if they know the service would not go on more than one hour."[6]

As unseemly as these examples might seem, there are other expressions of church-as-capitalist firm that are even more disturbing. Most troubling in many respects was the innovative legal argument put forward by Edward Egan, then the Catholic bishop of Bridgeport, Connecticut, in litigation several years ago. With eight of his priests accused of sexually abusing thirty young boys (the thirty now-grown men having sued the diocese), Bishop Egan—a canon lawyer by training—took a page from American corporate law in arguing that Catholic priests are not actually employees of the church, but rather are independent contractors for whom the employer is not liable in a legal sense.[7] This defense—used by corporations to avoid everything from paying Social Security taxes to massive legal judgments—was not definitively tested in court due to an out-of-court settlement of the case. Soon thereafter, Egan was promoted by the Vatican to his current position as Cardinal Archbishop of the Archdiocese of New York, where presumably he continues to oversee the work of thousands of independent contractors for whom he is not responsible in any legal or moral sense.

Jesus as Corporate Executive

Another example of the corporate penetration into church life is more decentralized and individualistic than these examples. It is found in the proliferation of books offered by publishing conglomerates that seek to derive "management lessons," "leadership insights," or "business wisdom" from Christian experience—most especially from the "life and teaching" of Jesus of Nazareth. While for years the evangelical subculture has produced a steady stream of "Jesus Wants You to Be Rich" and "How to Run A Christian Company and Make Money" books, more interesting here is the expansion of such Jesus-centered business and managerial self-help books beyond the evangelical market. Perhaps the quintessential example is Laurie Beth Jones, who leveraged her 1995 bestseller *Jesus CEO: Using Ancient Wisdom for Visionary Leadership*[8] into a wide-ranging management consulting, leadership training, and public seminar business targeting businesses, hospitals, government agencies, and nonprofit organizations. She now runs the Jesus CEO Foundation, publishes the *Jesus CEO News* (its motto is "Power You Can Use"), and has trained dozens of facilitators who now spread the Jesus CEO gospel via paid seminars, symposia, and conferences. The approach to business outlined in *Jesus CEO* has expanded via successor volumes to encompass a consulting/training function dedicated to constructing organizational mission statements and effective corporate management systems.

Jones has constructed an impressive edifice with her fellow "spiritreneurs"—a term of self-reference she created that means "highly talented and motivated" persons "who want to use our business talents and skills for the glory of God, yet remain independent from a bureaucracy." Despite the frequent mention of God in her newsletters (aimed at the true believers in her message), Jones's main book on Jesus and management is far from religious in tone or approach (its preface recommends the book to "any business, service, or endeavor that depends on more than one person to accomplish a goal").[9] The volume is a collection of short (mostly 2–4 page) chapters (with discussion questions at the end of each). Chapter titles describing Jesus' management style include "He Believed in Himself," "He Expressed Himself," "He Formed a Team," "He Took One Step at a Time," "He Was a Turnaround Specialist," "He Was Open to People and Their Ideas," and "He Clearly Defined Their Work-Related Benefits." The text is a painful combination of shallow sentiment, self-help clichés ("If only we believed in ourselves, the world would be a better place"), and trivialization of the Gospel accounts (she never answers the question of why Jesus drove moneychangers from the temple—among the most politically and theologically charged scenes in the entire New Testament—and instead changes it into a reflection on being a "passionate" leader).[10]

Like many other writers in the "Jesus the Business Hero" literature, Jones draws a highly stylized, individualistic, and decidedly Westernized portrait of Jesus. Ironically, a more forthright exposition of Jones's ideas on Christianity and capitalism is offered in an interview in *Industry Week*. She describes what initially attracted her to the topic: "I was struck by the fact that he had only three years to train 12 people—none of whom were divine—to go out and change the world; and that he trained them so effectively that they went on to do the work after he left. I asked, 'What did he do with these people to turn them into such lean, clean, marketing machines? What skills did he possess that we could duplicate or learn from?'"[11]

Out of the entire life and practice of Jesus, Jones distills three principles relevant to corporate management today: self-mastery, action, and relationship skills. Together these comprise the "Omega management style" used by Jesus, which "can be implemented by anyone who dares." These traits, she asserts, could readily fit many secular leaders like Jefferson, Edison, and Theodore Roosevelt. Furthermore, "Anyone who practices these spiritual principles is bound to experience success. In fact, the study and application of spiritual principles comes with success *guaranteed*."[12] Not even the crucifixion of Jesus—a political execution conducted by the bloody Roman Empire—is beyond utilization as a source of business boosterism and can-do thinking. As she says: "Jesus was such an action-oriented leader that they literally had to nail him down to keep him from doing more."[13]

God as Capitalist

Trying to figure out who or what God is is no easier now than it's ever been, hence the enduring appeal of negative methods focusing on what God is not. If it's well-nigh impossible to stipulate what God is, can we at least define what a capitalist is? Such looks to be a more manageable job for several reasons, but even here controversy is unavoidable. Values and ideology infuse all attempts to define capitalism and capitalists. Marx portrays the capitalist as a productive, albeit parasitic, force in historical development, while Michael Novak has gone so far as to compare the epitome of contemporary capitalism—the multinational corporation—to the Suffering Servant of the book of Isaiah, an appellation usually reserved in Christian theology for the Messiah.[14] By necessity, then, any stipulation of what a capitalist is can be examined for its biases, assumptions, and normative claims.

One advantage of living in a market culture like our own is that we all have been socialized into some widely shared notions of economic rationality, business logic, and a determinate range of what constitutes conventional business practice. Most of us recognize a constellation of practices, ideas, and norms that add up to "business as usual," and we can also recognize practices that extend, depart from, or violate those expectations—think again of Enron and other recent corporate miscreants. Given the limits of this essay, I will assume rather than demonstrate the existence of these shared ideas of capitalist practice and reasoning, fully acknowledging that these are social constructs with all the mutability, contestability, and divergent readings implied in the term. Whether I have adequately captured the mainstream social constructs of what capitalism is will be demonstrated, I suggest, by whether or not my sense of what capitalism means in our time and place accords with your and others' sense of the same.

Given all that, I remain convinced that whatever else God is, God is not a capitalist. To anticipate one line of objection, neither is God a state socialist (though that argument will not be made here). There are several reasons why it seems that God-as-capitalist misperceives the person of God, the mission of Jesus, and the ways in which God engages with his good-but-fallen creation.

First and foremost, from a capitalist point of view, God has a lousy business model. Consider the parable about hiring workers for the vineyard at different times of the day and paying them all the same wage (Matt. 20:1–16). Any businessperson reading this as a straightforward description would conclude the obvious: there's no way in which this is an economically competitive practice. Overpaying the latecomers results in a wage bill higher than one's competitors; no extra payments for the all-day laborers invites resentment and its sequelae—shirking, sabotage, and more. It also provides no material incentives for working hard, for loyalty to the boss, for reliability. It's bad labor utilization and is certain to put God's vineyard out of business sooner rather than later. It looks like another satire by those people at *The Onion*.

Or consider the shepherd who leaves ninety-nine sheep to retrieve a lost one (Matt. 18:12–14). It's an admirable sentiment, of course, but bad business practice. While the Good Shepherd is out retrieving that lost lamb, the rest of the flock is left unprotected—the best might be wooed away by a competing shepherd, and wolves might attack and deplete your inventory of mutton. It's also a move that callously disregards the reality of opportunity costs—time spent looking for that one sheep might be better spent increasing the size of the flock, building some fencing for the pasture, or diversifying out of sheep only and into vineyard cultivation—especially if one's neighboring vineyard owner seems intent on bankrupting himself by overpaying on wages and benefits. Every investor accepts a certain percentage of imperfection or loss in processes of production, transport, inventory, and sales—sheep are interchangeable, after all, at least from the perspective of those whose interest in them is coterminous with their shearing or butchering. The Good Shepherd needs to appreciate the importance of a productive level of wastage, in other words, and stop getting so personally invested in individual lambs. Just as an employer can't get too close to employees he or she may someday need to lay off, it's bad shepherding to get hung up about a single sheep.

Or consider another aspect of God's personnel policy—on more than one occasion God seems determined to call the halt and the lame, the poor and the marginal (see for example Luke 14:12–14). While there is a certain amount of public relations benefit to be had—one gets points for being a socially responsible corporation by hiring the "differently abled," of course—nobody in his or her right mind would build a firm around these sorts of folks. It ignores the central importance in our time of human capital formation, creativity, and training—you need top-shelf people to master technology, innovate often, and keep their skills packages up to world-class levels. The "least of these"[15]—or the least of these employees—can't possibly compete, can't possibly maximize shareholder value, and can't possibly make for a rational human resources strategy. God might well like the "stone the builder rejected"[16] but you can't minimize the importance of high-quality materials, human and otherwise, in building a world-class firm.

Or consider the promise that the gospel makes to the followers of Jesus: "as they did to me they will do to you" (and variations thereof, e.g., Mark 13:7–13, Luke 9:23–26). It's not going out on a limb, I suggest, to say that if you promise persecution and maybe martyrdom for those who get your corporate message *right*—well, that just is not a very attractive benefits package. You won't be able to attract the best people, you won't be able to motivate them to work hard and with loyalty—a career ladder shaped like a cross is not going to work. It's a bad idea all the way around.

There are just so many signs that God has a bad business plan. Every time he moves to affirm that "the last shall be first and the first shall be last," he scares away would-be investors, loses market share, and pushes the most ambitious persons out of the firm. Elton Mayo may have built a kinder, gentler school of labor utilization around the touchy-feely type of human relations (use compliments instead of threats, treat your workers well and they'll work well for you, and all that), but you can't put the last first and the first last. The last are last for a reason—they're too stupid, or not sufficiently ruthless, or carrying too much baggage from prior exploitation or victimization. And if you don't put the first on top you're violating the natural order, setting up perverse incentives, and thwarting the evolution of better ideas, more efficient sorts of activities, and the creation of wealth.

These are just a few of the bad business practices that God, through Jesus, implements in the Gospels. But this isn't the entire story. Consider the strategies that God and Jesus don't practice that are part and parcel of every capitalist enterprise. God not only does things guaranteed to frustrate economic rationality, God passes up other things that constitute good stewardship of economic resources and the production of value.

Consider, for example, the whole question of incentives. Contemporary capitalism lives in a world in which political entities offer incentives—tax breaks, subsidies, regulatory exemptions—to attract capitalist investment in one community rather than another. Illinois competes with Kentucky, the United States with Germany, Haiti with Honduras—while some people call corporate incentives a form of legal bribery, they're an important part of what every good capitalist considers in making investment decisions.

But not God. Not only does God seem decidedly lukewarm toward some traditional forms of incentives (burnt offerings and sacrifices, for example), God doesn't seem attuned to locating where maximal return could be obtained. With all due respect to God's site location team, choosing a backwater like Galilee as the site for the incarnation seems remarkably short-sighted: doubtless the Romans would have offered a much more attractive package of temple construction, tax subsidies, and legal privileges were divinity to come in the form of the emperor (for real, not just in pagan terms) or some other imperial notable. But Galilee? Bad transportation infrastructure, far from major religious markets, distant from suppliers, and not likely to jump from an ethnic/niche market within Judaism to a worldwide commodity.

God also doesn't lay off enough people. One mainstay of the stock market bubble of the 1990s was the creative use of layoffs to boost stock prices. AT&T laid off 40,000 people one week and saw its stock price soar; many other companies did the same thing. Cutting payroll means lower costs, which means the prospect for higher dividends for owners—hence a more attractive position in the stock market.

But what does God do? Does God lay off unproductive followers? Does God build around a core of permanent, full-time followers and hire and fire temporary Christians at will?

It would seem to be a more efficient system were God to do so—but here again, God doesn't take advantage of some obvious, market-rational opportunities. Prostitutes and tax collectors might well be able to bring in some revenue for the divine enterprise here on earth, but lepers, cripples, orphans, and widows don't add much to the bottom line. Let 'em go—if things pick up, maybe we'll call them back. But right now they are low-yield, high-cost parts of the organization, so they have to go. But does God do that, or make similar reductions in force that would make Christianity look like a religion on the way up, a bandwagon to jump upon? Apparently not.

God obviously is not as smart as even the average capitalist. For God seems unaware that, given this sort of business plan, God will go bankrupt—nobody can continue by giving people more than what they produce, by privileging the weak and the inefficient over the strong and the powerful, by ignoring those with resources to give in favor of those who have nothing and amount to nothing. Jesus passed up countless money-making opportunities—he didn't charge for healings, he gave loaves and fishes by the thousands (angering the bakery owners' association and the fishing industry in the process), and he alienated a rich young man who might have otherwise bankrolled the ministry. Either God wasn't being literal in ways binding on the church in these matters—our preferred interpretation of these and many other parts of the scriptural tradition—or else God needs sober-minded lower managers to protect God's patrimony from God's overly generous heart. That would be our job, of course, helping to impose some realism and rationality on God's interaction with the world, lest God's creation be undone by the goodness of God's own heart. Many corporations have a kindly founder or figurehead who epitomizes charity and sweetness, after all, with an army of functionaries below him or her who make the real decisions based on the hard realities of the marketplace and our fallen world. God needs to be protected from God's own self—thank God that God has us.

But what if God doesn't want protection? What if bankruptcy of a sort is itself essential to God's plan of salvation?

Let me explain. Not being content to wallow in the richness of divine power, God chooses to empty God's own self in the incarnation (see Phil. 2:7). This incarnation of Jesus is a radical emptying, a squandering of power and privilege and metaphysical riches—at least that is how it appears from our human point of view. For our sake, God did not choose a plan to maximize God's honor and glory and adulation, but rather a stripping away of divine favor and privilege. God-become-human looks like bankruptcy voluntarily chosen to save humanity from itself and its sinfulness.

Similarly, the death and resurrection of Jesus looks like a transcendent expression of debt forgiveness—rather than leaving us with the debts of sin and evil we so richly and fully earned for ourselves, God raised Jesus from the dead and in so doing forgave us all of our IOUs, all our just desserts, the wages of sin due us in any rational accounting of good and evil (see Rom. 6:23). Just as Yahweh instituted a radical, this-worldly form of debt forgiveness in the Jubilee practices of Israel—intending to eradicate debt every seven years, returning land lost through debt and bondage every forty-nine years—so God offers an even more radical form of Jubilee forgiveness of debts in the death and resurrection of Jesus.[17] This sort of forgiveness cannot but look like a short road to bankruptcy from a capitalist point of view.[18]

With this notion of bankruptcy in mind, I think we're now in position to examine the parable that most often finds its way into justifications for the harmony of Christianity and capitalism. I'm referring, of course, to the parable of the talents (Matt. 25:14–30), in which a man going on a journey gives money to his servants and then returns to settle accounts. This parable is so familiar to us that we think we know who is who when we hear it. I won't presume that centuries of capitalism and its formative processes have shaped our reading of this parable, but of course it is common sense that God is the owner of the estate, that the servants to admire are those who increased the value of God's property, and that the servant to be criticized is the one who didn't multiply his master's wealth and instead buried his capital. Of course that's how we should read this parable.

And yet, what if we shift the terms of reference just slightly to bring them more in line with the actual processes of wealth acquisition in first-century Palestine? Consider the implications if:

- the master of the estate is not God, but Satan;
- the servant who defies the master is not a lazy freeloader, but is Jesus himself?

Why, then the parable takes a more dramatic turn, one more in keeping with the lived experience of wealth and poverty relations in poor countries (and in some of our own practices). If, in fact, the master is not God, then the Old Testament presumption that most wealth represents the subsistence of the poor taken by the rich comes back into play. If the wealth left with the servants is not a gift from God but instead is the product of previous exploitation of the orphaned and widowed (note the unmistakable Old Testament references here in "reaping where he doesn't sow, and gathering where he does not scatter"), then what is asked of the servants is to generate still more wealth by still more exploitation. Most likely, the path to a good return on the invested talents used Palestinian poverty as a context for loans given under extortionate terms, bringing either high rates of return, foreclosed land, or both. How else could one obtain these outrageous rates of return—100 percent, a doubling—in a premodern agrarian setting?[19] It seems strange, after all, to ascribe to God the axiom "to those who have, more will be given, while those who have nothing, even what they have will be given away" (Matt. 25:29)—a first-century phrasing of our more common adage, "The rich get richer and the poor get poorer."

And what if the disobedient servant is one who refuses to save himself by adding to the misery of those even worse off than himself, one who is willing to lose everything rather than generate wealth on the backs of the poor? This servant willingly accepts bankruptcy, abandonment, and suffering rather than engage in economic practices that rob others of their means of subsistence and provisioning. He is a Suffering Servant in the true sense, contrary to Michael Novak's use of the term for multinational corporations. What a different picture results from adjusting just two assumptions—assumptions neither required nor invited by the gospel itself, but seemingly essential to our market-centered way of thinking and living. What a bad capitalist God turns out to be.

The Economics of the Kingdom

Steve Long argues that a fundamental difference between the Christian God and capitalism is that God presumes plenitude and abundance, and capitalism presumes—and creates—scarcity.[20] For many people this discussion ends by invoking the fall—all that plenitude and abundance was left behind in the Garden of Eden thanks to sin, replaced by work and the sweat of one's brow in an endless struggle to survive (see Gen. 3:19).

Looking only at the beginning of the story is often a dead end. What is needed is a reclaimed and lively *eschatology*—a Christian vision of the end—that ties economic practices to the church. That is, we need to think about our economics in terms of what the church is called to be as a foretaste and forerunner of the kingdom of God. While some of us have begun making preliminary incursions into what the economic implications of the church as harbinger of the kingdom might include, it is clearly an area in need of development by theologians, pastors and lay church leaders, and Christian scholars from many disciplines.

The most pressing need, it seems to me, is to begin the long and difficult process of freeing our theological and ecclesial imaginations. Our notions of economy, church, realism, and the like are so deeply infused with market-centered assumptions that most creative work is doomed from the outset. While we're now beginning to gain some traction in seeing the church as a distinctive form of community instituted by God to continue Jesus' work of the kingdom, we need also to think of the church as having its own economy, its own exemplary and real-world practices, ideas, and theologies of provision, property, and prosperity.

Let me conclude with one illustration that can only be suggestive rather than definitive. Time and again many parts of the Christian tradition have returned to the Sermon on the Mount (Matt. 5–7) to think afresh about matters of church, power, and mission. What if we look to the Sermon as a source of ideas on Christian economic practices as well? If God is not a capitalist, then God's church ought not be capitalist either. Perhaps the Sermon on the Mount, called by Augustine "a summary of the whole gospel,"[21] can free our imaginations to conceive a noncapitalist church and a noncapitalist God. The Sermon on the Mount joins together the upside-down blessings of the Beatitudes, the Lord's Prayer, the "lilies of the field," and the Golden Rule. It contains the most important "hard sayings" of Jesus—loving one's enemies, repaying evil with good, putting aside material worries, and rejoicing in persecution and suffering. Putting aside the many forms of evasion of the Sermon found in Christian history—there are Catholic and Protestant variants developed in abundance—this "magna carta" of the Christian way can give cues and tastes for those prepared to receive them.

For example, Matthew 5:17–48 contains a variety of ways in which Jesus intensifies, deepens, and expands the best sense of the Jewish law. With the kingdom having broken through in the person and proclamation of Jesus, the law's concessions to human limitation and sin are removed. Jesus and the Holy Spirit are all the help we need now to begin living the law's best intent without reservation, loopholes, or evasion. Where the law prohibited murder, Jesus now proscribes anger and resentment. The ban on adulterous behavior extends now to adulterous and possessive desire. Revenge, oath-taking, divorce, conduct with enemies—Jesus radicalizes them all so that God's desires for humanity can now be pursued without dilution—beginning in the life and practice of the church, the first bit of reclaimed territory in the human community.

The economic implications here are manifest in that the Sermon also intends, I suggest, that the church adapt the economic practices of Israel—notably Sabbath and its social expression, the Jubilee—in the here and now. When using the Sermon as a starting point for an economics for discipleship, one begins with dangerous but potentially fruitful materials—practices of distributing wealth instead of hoarding it, resisting the temptation toward individualized strategies of economic security in favor of trusting in the bounty of God, and a regular forgiveness of debt and redistribution of productive property.

Consider Matthew 5:42: "Give to anyone who asks you." Jesus calls upon his disciples to practice an economics of abundance—to imitate the profligate generosity of God, who gives generously to all humanity regardless of merit (which is why God has a lousy labor utilization policy, you may recall). The presumption that abundance rather than scarcity forms the basis of creation distinguishes Christianity from all secular schools of economics, in which scarcity is the foundational assumption.[22]

Consider the Lord's Prayer, in which the disciples are instructed to pray for *daily* bread—not unlimited bread, not a month's worth, not control of the bread market, not a storage facility for surplus bread, but *daily* bread—trusting that God will provide for God's people just as Yahweh provided manna for Israel in the desert. In return for God's daily fidelity and generosity, disciples are instructed to pray for, and to practice, debt forgiveness—inaugurating Jubilee practices among themselves in the here and now. In this way, they become an unmistakable light for the world (5:15), and a sign that in fact the kingdom has come because Yahweh's will is now being done on earth as presumably it has always been done in heaven (6:10). Such economic practices are demanding and are not likely to be popular choices (7:13–14), but they are essential to Jesus' purposes of announcing the in-breaking of God's kingdom, standing as a beacon inviting others into God's new day, and being good news to the poor.

Finally, it may well be the case that the Sermon's key contribution to an economics of discipleship comes from 6:25–33—the well-known but relentlessly spiritualized "lilies of the field" passage. Here are outrageous promises, offering to those who seek and live in the kingdom and in the justice it brings marvelous plenitude and freedom from the anxiety that scarcity produces. But in a world in which billions go hungry, in which millions of children die too soon while the wealthy gorge themselves, what has happened to these promises? Does God not keep God's word?

The promises remain valid, I suggest, and God remains ready to deliver as promised. Thus far, however, these promises have been thwarted by our unwillingness—the church's unwilling-ness—to live "thy Kingdom come." We in the church block the promises by still being slaves who put our trust in money and our personal wealth (6:24). Because we have not trusted in God's abundance, and because we have not risked our security by trusting the new brothers and sisters given to us by God, the outrageous promises of God are choked off and burn like cruel, impossible dreams, when in fact we have frustrated the preconditions for their fulfillment from the outset.

This brief excursion into the Sermon on the Mount just scratches the surface of God's radical economy. Yet I hope it has been sufficient to give a taste of what God is like and what the church might become in matters economic. Getting be-yond notions of a capitalist God served by a capitalist church would be one necessary step in bringing those promises closer to fulfillment.

5

God Is
Not Religious

William T. Cavanaugh

The chapter titles in this book are intended to be jarring and provocative. We all know that to get an audience these days you have to be shocking, so we have put together the theological equivalent of the *Jerry Springer Show*. The title I got stuck with, however, seems rather unprovocative and common. "God is not religious" is a sentiment one hears quite regularly from the most ordinary of folk. First, it reflects a common prejudice against organization and institutions. "Organized religion" is a term that registers on the scale of what is cool somewhere between "Brussels sprouts" and "orthopedic shoes." I was working as a pizza cook in high school the first time somebody told me "God doesn't live in a church." What he seemed to mean was "I like to sleep in on Sunday." But he was expressing a dominant sentiment of popular culture: God is most readily accessible to the individual acting on his or her own.

Second, the "God is not religious" sentiment reflects the common claim "I'm spiritual, but not religious." Religion seems to denote crabbed dogmatism, bureaucratic sclerosis, and dead ritual. Spirituality, on the other hand, seems to offer freedom, vitality, and a direct encounter with the divinity of one's choice without the intervention of any other person. Celebrities parade their spirituality on talk television, and publishers cash in on a booming how-to-be-spiritual market.

Nevertheless, I have no intention of confirming the common wisdom. I do not like Brussels sprouts, but I am a big fan of the "organized" part of "organized religion." To be against organized religion is like being against organized hospitals. I am going to criticize the concept of "religion," but not in order to vindicate "spirituality." In fact, I think spirituality is just an extension of what is wrong with religion. And what is wrong with religion is not that it is organized, but that it, like spirituality, has been used to turn faith in God into a consumer item for our private consolation and amusement. So, I hope to end up being provocative after all. When I claim that God is not religious, I mean to say that "religion," like "spirituality," has been used to privatize Christian practice, marginalize it from common life, bury God deep within the confines of the individual self, and thereby turn the individual over to the disciplines and designs of the nation-state and the market. In other words, the term "religion" has been part and parcel of the trivialization of God in our society.

To show all of this, I will first do a short genealogy of the word "religion"; tracing the changes in a word's meaning helps to free us from the sense that its present meaning is necessary or unchangeable. In the next three sections, I will show how the concept of religion has been used to facilitate the interiorization, privatization, and relativization of the Christian faith. Finally, I will end with some reflections on how faith in the living God helps us lose our religion. These five sections involve a bit of intellectual history—the discussion of thinkers and movements and events that may not be familiar to everyone. Though it may seem to be at first glance, this discussion isn't the least bit academic and esoteric. Rather, it is the story of how religion in our society has tried to show God the door.

Genealogy of "Religion"

The meanings of words change and adapt to meet new circumstances. Words do not exist in dictionaries but in real-life exchanges among living people. The dictionary struggles to keep up with adaptations, adding new words and meanings and marking others as archaic. In the case of religion, variations on the word have been around for millennia, but the way we use the word today is relatively new. Its rise accompanied new arrangements in power in Europe and the world, arrangements that posed, and still pose, significant challenges for the Christian church.

The word derives from the Latin *religio,* a minor term that did not originally mean what we take religion to mean today. *Religio* referred to a binding obligation (from *re + ligare,* to rebind); to say that something was *"religio* to me" meant that it represented a special obligation. The term referred not just to cults of the gods but also oaths and family obligations, things we would think of as "secular." When Christians began to spread throughout the Roman Empire, the word had very little importance, mostly because it didn't translate any one concept that the Christians considered important. In the official Latin version of the New Testament, the Vulgate, *religio* appeared only six times, as translation for several different Greek terms. In the King James Version of the New Testament, "religion" appears only five times, to translate three different Greek terms, not always the same ones the Vulgate renders *religio.*[1] Only one ancient Christian writer, Saint Augustine, wrote a treatise on *religio.* He uses the term to mean roughly what we mean when we say "worship," including "secular" uses of the term, such as "He worships money." Whether a certain practice of *religio* is true or false depends on its object, which can be anything from the one true God to mere material things.[2] In the medieval period, no one seems to have bothered to focus an entire treatise on *religio*. In his magisterial *Summa Theologica*, Thomas Aquinas devoted only one question out of over six hundred to *religio*.

When the term is used in the premodern period, it tends to refer either to the state of being under monastic vows or to a particular virtue shared by all Christians. In Aquinas's discussion of *religio* in the *Summa*, it refers both to what we would call the piety of the Christian and to the liturgical practices through which piety is directed to God; that is, it refers both to our devotion to God and to our acts of devotion, like communal prayer and Eucharist. Aquinas devotes an article to showing that *religio* includes a bodily act. This is important, because for Aquinas and the medieval church there is no separation between interior piety and the ritual actions that express this piety. There is no separation of body and soul: the soul is disciplined through the body, and the body expresses what is in the soul. Thus a virtue is a bodily habit. Furthermore, *religio* is not an individual thing. It is a virtue engaged in the communal liturgical practices—the ways of worship—of the church.

When the term passed into English around 1200, it referred to monastic life in general. But in the next couple of centuries the meaning would be expanded to include a notion of plurality: the "religions" of England were the various Christian orders—Benedictine, Franciscan, Dominican, etc.[3] This, of course, has very little to do with our modern idea that Christianity is itself a religion, one species of a genus of things that includes Islam, Buddhism, and Baha'i. As we have also seen, religion before modernity is nothing like the kind of private, interior experience that it will become in modernity. At this point in time, however, a radically new idea of religion is about to emerge, just as the modern state and capitalism burst on the scene. This is not a coincidence.

Interiorization

The origin of the modern concept of religion can be seen clearly in the thought of two fifteenth-century Christian Platonist thinkers, Nicholas of Cusa and Marsilio Ficino. For Cusa, religion is identified not with rites or bodily practices but with an essence that stands behind the practices. The body interfered with true religion. What was needed was "that man would have to walk according to his interior rather than his exterior nature."[4] The "interior man" was one who relied on reason, not the senses: "all who use their reason have one religion and cult which is at the bottom of all the diversity of rites."[5] This bottom, for Cusa, was still Christian; the common essence of religion was in reality faith in Christ. But it is a different Christianity, because his conception of religion interiorizes a "real" core that is distinguished from "mere" external actions (like the church's worship). That is new.

Ficino took up this theme and claimed that religion is an innate human impulse planted by God in the hearts of all without need of special revelation. Unlike Cusa's view that some rites (Christian rites) were better than others, Ficino had a more positive view of the diversity of rites. He saw this variety as ordained by God to give beauty to the world. As such, however, they are mere ornamentation. The real thing, the essence of religion, is worshiping God in one's heart. The highest form of religion is worshiping God as Christ did.[6]

The next step in the invention of interiorized religion comes in the sixteenth century, when religion comes to be understood as a set of doctrines to be believed. Some scholars note this change in the meaning of "religion" already in Calvin's work in the sixteenth century; others say it does not occur until Calvin's successors have interpreted his work. What is clear is that by the time the Calvinist Hugo Grotius wrote *De Veritate Religionis Christianae* in the early seventeenth century, he was able to say that the Christian religion *teaches*, rather than simply *is*, the correct worship of God.

The addition of "the" to "Christian religion" is highly significant as well. Christianity is now a religion, understood as a system of doctrines. And since there have been several such systems elaborated among human peoples, it is now possible to speak of "religions" in the plural.[7] This change from religion as a virtue to religion as doctrine is very significant, for it limits the range of Christian faith from the entire body of the believer to the space between the ears. Faith for Aquinas was a virtue, and therefore a type of bodily habit to be practiced; in the modern era, faith would come increasingly to be seen as an interior attitude of receptiveness to a set of doctrinal propositions.

Religion would continue to be located "within" the individual, but the emphasis on doctrine would fade in the thought of many of the new theorists of religion. In the early seventeenth century, for example, Lord Herbert of Cherbury located religion in a faculty of the mind known as "natural instinct."[8] Truth in religion was available to all people through the exercise of this mental instinct. Lord Herbert distilled all world religions down to a simple and virtually contentless piety innate in all humans. Unlike in Cusa and Ficino, Christ did not provide the key to true and proper piety; Christ was merely an exemplary teacher of true religion. Indeed, all "outward expressions" beyond the simple worship of "God" and the acknowledgement of our sins were to be regarded with suspicion as priestly additions to pure religion. True religion is without a church, without doctrines, without discipline or formation through bodily practices. Lord Herbert made room for revelation in his scheme, but revelation was validated only by appeal to inward emotional states, the "intimate divine apprehensions" whereby we "feel within us His saving power and a sense of marvellous deliverance."[9]

Here Lord Herbert anticipates the next step in making the concept of religion even more gaseous; the essence of religion would come to be located not in rational thought but in feeling. The great figure of this movement is the nineteenth-century founder of liberal Protestantism, Friedrich Schleiermacher. For Schleiermacher, the essence of religion was neither thought nor action, but feeling and intuition. The highest experience of religion was a deep, immediate apprehension of oneness between the individual and the infinite—a "feeling of absolute dependence." Schleiermacher did not thereby dispense with revelation, for he was convinced that the ability to name this feeling as religious only came from the knowledge of a particular tradition of doctrine and practice. That is, Schleiermacher could name this experience as an experience of God only because he had been given this language by the Christian tradition.[10] Nevertheless, in Schleiermacher religion is firmly based in individual experience and is identified with something essentially nonrational. God has been fully interiorized, buried deep in the recesses of the individual heart.

It is a short step, therefore, from religion to the kind of spirituality that infests popular culture today. Although church attendance is down 12 percent over the last decade alone, publishers have dubbed that same time period the "decade of the soul." For example, witness the growing market share of the *Chicken Soup for the Soul* phenomenon, now in its *6th Bowl,* with niche titles for the golfer's soul, the NASCAR soul, the pet lover's soul, and so on, with crossover products in video, music, and toys.[11] For this brand of spirituality, God is a coping mechanism, a kind of "divine Prozac."[12] People pick and choose their own gods, though often without acknowledging it. These gods are not "out there," a reality in the universe that reveals itself to us, but rather "in here," small and available to fulfill our wants. As one devotee of such spirituality told the *Washington Post,* "We discovered the God within. That's why we need God. Because we are God."[13] Of course, this shrinking of God down to the confines of the self is not what Schleiermacher had in mind. But this type of feel-good spirituality represents only the logical extension of the interiorization of religion.

Privatization

Once religion is driven inward, it becomes relatively easy, and appears inevitable, that it should also be driven out of public life. Consider this quote from Schleiermacher: "Religion

. . . in its own original, characteristic form, is not accustomed to appear openly, but is only seen in secret by those who love it."[14] Religion, in other words, should be felt but not seen. Religion in modernity, because individual and nonrational, has been separated out from the public domain and made a private concern. We are accustomed to seeing this process as inevitable, a sifting out of two essentially distinct things—the religious and the secular—that had previously been confused. As we have seen, however, religion was not simply there to be separated out like metal from its ore. Religion was *invented* as a necessary adjunct to new forms of political and economic power. In order for the state to emerge in modernity, it would be necessary to remove the church from the public domain. The new concept of religion was integral to this process.

Secularization, therefore, is not just a separating out of the religious from the secular but the invention of a whole new conception of society, one in which God would rule hearts and minds, but not bodies—and certainly not visible political and economic processes. To see the difference, all we have to do is compare "secular" in early Christianity and modernity. For traditional Christianity, the *saeculum* was not a space but a time, the time between the fall and the second coming of Christ. During this time, certain instruments of power, guided by divine providence, were necessary to restrain sin. In the modern era, by contrast, the secular is not a time but a space, a supposedly neutral space outside the influence of "religion." The secular is an autonomous space, ruled by sheer arbitrary power, in which politics may carry on as if God did not exist.[15]

It was not always so. In the traditional Christian worldview, there was no human activity that fell outside of the workings of divine providence. Marriage, economic activity, charitable foundations, relationships of kinship, festivals and celebrations, political institutions, and death were all enfolded into the liturgical life of the church. All of these relationships and activities were, of course, fraught with conflict, and they were rarely fully just or completely loving. But the point is that there was as yet no formal attempt to separate power from love using the logic of public-private or secular-sacred dualities. There was, in other words, no attempt to confine the activity of God to a private sphere so that the machinations of the human will could operate without interference.[16]

This ended with the advent of modernity, when the state took over and shoved the church aside. In the medieval era, civil authority was regarded as the "police department of the church."[17] Beginning at least in the fourteenth century, however, the civil authority began to assert its own independence from the church. By Luther's time, civil rulers had already substantially taken over the church's right to appoint bishops and abbots and had taken control of church revenues in many countries. Both Catholic and Protestant rulers were intent on taking over power from the church. Luther's theory of the two kingdoms, then, was not really such a new idea, but responded to the aspirations of princes, both Catholic and Protestant, to rule without church interference. Luther taught that every Christian is simultaneously subject to two kingdoms, the temporal and the spiritual. To the temporal powers, kings and princes, the power of coercion over bodies has been given in order to keep the civil peace in a world full of sinners. To the spiritual power, the church, has been given only the Word of God for the persuasion of souls; ecclesiastical courts, for example, were eliminated. The net result was that the church became the province of souls; bodies were handed over to the emergent state.[18]

At first the powerful new modern state would continue to take on sacred duties. Eventually, the state would become secularized. Either way, however, the state became the primary focus of the individual's public allegiance, and the church became increasingly privatized. As John Neville Figgis comments, by the close of the sixteenth century, "the religion of the State has replaced the religion of the Church, or, to be more correct, that religion is becoming individual while the civil power is recognized as having the paramount claims of an organized society upon the allegiance of its members. . . . [T]he essence of their position is to treat the unity of the State as the paramount end, to which unity in religion must give way."[19]

Once the state has gained a monopoly on making rules for human society, and once religion has been defined as a private, individual matter for the soul, it does not really matter if the state claims to be sacred or secular. The fact remains that the state is the only thing worth dying for and the only thing worth killing for. The United States has a secular constitutional arrangement with a separation between church and state. Crucial to this separation is the distinction between body and soul, conduct and "mere belief." Thomas Jefferson "held that 'operations of the mind' are not subject to legal coercion, but that 'acts of the body' are. 'Mere belief,' said Jefferson, 'in one god or 20, neither picks one's pockets nor breaks one's legs.'"[20] Religion should be free, therefore, between the ears, as long as the rest of the body is prepared to let the state pick its pockets and break its legs. It does not much matter what we believe, as long as we are willing to support the next war with our money and our bodies, to dutifully go and kill whomever the state tells us to kill.

This does not mean that religion has disappeared from the scene. Poll-takers still tell us that the United States is one of the most religious countries in the world, where 90 percent of people still say they believe in some sort of supreme being or beings. What we see, however, is a society in which what we do on Sundays does not have much effect on what goes on Monday through Friday. Religion is still occasionally trotted out in public to provide an aura of legitimacy for whatever we were going to do anyway, fighting wars especially. For the most part, however, religion in public is what we object to most strenuously about our enemies. The "clash of civilizations" we are currently witnessing, we are told, is between the civil and tolerant West that has learned to treat religion as a private leisure activity and the Muslim world that is brimming with fanaticism because they keep letting religion out in public.[21] Religion is seen as essentially nonrational and therefore prone to irrationality. Killing for religion is crazy; killing for access to cheap oil is okey-dokey.

The invention of religion as a private leisure activity allows people to fit into the state and the market without conflict.

When Jesus tells us in Matthew 6:24 "You cannot serve both God and mammon," we quickly add "on the same day." On Sunday we take a break from corporate life to praise Jesus, even if the Salvadoran girls we pay forty cents an hour to make our shoes have to work on the Sabbath. Private religion is meant as a refuge, solace for tired shoppers and harried office workers. Religion helps us escape from or cope with, but not change, the frenetic pace of life in a consumer society.

We have seen how the concept "religion" was invented in the modern era to marginalize the church and facilitate the rise of the state and capitalism. It is crucial to see, however, that the privatization of religion is not simply inevitable, some type of evolutionary process to which we simply must bow. Let me illustrate. Several years ago, while staying with my godparents in Winona, Minnesota, I discovered an old geography textbook of the kind that used to be used in Catholic middle schools in this country. The publication date in the book is 1952. The chapters on economics are a wonder to behold. Under the heading, "Sharing Goods through Trade," the book has the following characterization of economic life as mediated through the medieval guilds. "The Just Price for each article was arrived at by the Guildsmen themselves. Cost of production, fair wages for workers, and a decent profit for the seller were considered, and balanced against the fair price which people could pay for their necessities."[22] Piling up great fortunes, we are told, was frowned upon, for money was to be regarded as merely on loan from God. Today, however, the textbook says indignantly,

> Few people dream that it is wrong to get as much as you can for what you sell, and to beat down a seller to as cheap a price as he will take, regardless of the Just Price. Products often sell today according to "supply and demand.". . . Prices change continually, giving one man wealth without his deserving it and ruining another through no fault of his own. What is worse, unscrupulous men often manage the market for their own benefit.[23]

The root of the problem, the textbook teaches, is that

> in American business life, religion is not a great power. Even
> Catholics have largely lost the sense of obeying Christ in ev-
> eryday life. Church is too often thought to be for Sunday, and
> religion is limited to saying one's prayers; so long as a man does
> not murder or commit adultery, he thinks he is on God's side.
> This is a sad result of today's unreligious surroundings.[24]

But the textbook does not merely lament. It gives detailed accounts of contemporary businesspeople who do conduct their businesses according to the principle of the Just Price: farmers, barterers, small manufacturers, co-operatives, and others.[25] Today we might cite such examples as "Fair Trade" coffee, whereby people voluntarily pay higher prices for coffee in order to ensure a living wage to growers in Third World countries.

Despite the overly romanticized nostalgia for the twelfth century, this textbook is remarkable for its refusal to accept the privatization of religion in the twentieth century. The textbook unblinkingly teaches the basic incompatibility of privatized religion with the gospel, and it sees quite clearly that such an arrangement is not inevitable. Indeed, the textbook itself is evidence that it is not inevitable, because it is evidence that Christian education can quite willfully transgress the boundaries between the gospel and economics that the modern concept of religion helps to construct. Unfortunately, the fate of this textbook is evidence of the kind of privatization we have been discussing. Catholic schools no longer use this type of textbook. Catholic schools today largely use the same geography textbooks that the public schools are using, on the tacit assumption that God has nothing distinctive or relevant to say about economics and other such "secular" matters. Only the religion textbooks are distinctively Christian. Insofar as Christianity is thus quarantined in religion classes, however, we may wonder if what we are teaching our kids is distinctively Christian at all or simply another variant of privatized religion.

Relativization

The interiorization and privatization of Christianity expressed by the new concept of religion are accompanied by a third change, that of relativization. As you recall, from the fifteenth to the seventeenth century religion went from naming a particular virtue attached to the liturgical rites of the church to a universal impulse implanted in the hearts of all peoples. It was then possible to think of religion as something that every human person had access to, with or without revelation. The revelation of Jesus Christ may have taught humans the highest form of religion, as Ficino thought, or may have confirmed the deepest wells of personal religious experience, as Lord Herbert thought, but religion as such is native to the human heart and precedes Christ or any objective revelation. Later, the term "religion" comes to refer to the various rites and systems of belief through which different peoples express this universal impulse. This makes it possible to speak of "religions" in the plural. As a consequence, each religion came to be seen as an expression of the basic essence of religion as such. Religion is the genus, of which Christianity is one species, along with Buddhism, Judaism, Shinto, Islam, Confucianism, Hinduism, and so on.

In the eighteenth and nineteenth centuries, this new definition of religion became a useful tool in the hands of European colonial powers. They defined "religion" according to Christian ideas and practice; a religion had a god or gods, creeds, Scriptures, organized worship, hierarchical authority, and other features that allowed it to be properly differentiated from culture, economics, politics, and other secular activities. Other cultural systems such as "Hinduism" (the word was invented in the nineteenth century) were categorized as "religions." Then, since Hinduism did not look much like Christianity—lacking creeds and church and largely undifferentiated from culture in general—Hinduism was judged a "primitive" form of religion. This was very useful for justifying colonial domination. The work of the colonial powers would be advanced as an elevating and civilizing influence on the primitive practitioners of primitive religions. Friedrich Max Mueller, the famed godfather of the study of world religions, was instrumental in systematizing Western research into Hinduism in the nineteenth century. It is not a coincidence that his work in India was financed by the British East India Company, one of the principal arms of British imperial rule.[26]

In one sense we are long past this crude religious imperialism. Indeed, now the idea that Christianity is one religion among many religions is more commonly used to the exact opposite effect, the relativization of Christ as just one path among many, all of equal value. In academic circles the most prominent exponent of this view has been John Hick, who advocates a model in which each religion is just one way up the mountain to what he calls Ultimate Reality. In the face of this absolute Ultimate Reality, all particular religions must be relativized, that is, seen not as absolute truth in themselves, but mere pointers to the absolute truth, which remains mysterious—unspeakable or even unknowable. All revelations are seen as partial revelations, never expressing the fullness of the absolute. Christ then, like Mohammed or the Buddha, can only be seen as a pointer to something else, and not as in himself the way, the truth, and the life. Truth is one, but it has many names, none of which exhaust the mystery. All the great world religions can lead to Ultimate Reality. None of them can claim that the revelation on which they are based is uniquely privileged over other revelations.[27]

Once such diverse sets of practices and beliefs as Christianity, Confucianism, Hinduism, and Shinto get lumped together as so many religions sharing a common essence, they are seen as competitors in the same field. Hick and the other religious pluralists believe they have found a way to celebrate the uniqueness of each religion without trying to assert the superiority of one over the others. This they believe will encourage peaceful understanding in our globalized world. This is not just an academic solution, but one I hear often from my students and the proverbial man or woman on the street. We like to think we are being inclusive and tolerant by saying that all religions are really just the same underneath all the rites and beliefs. The solution doesn't work, however, because instead of asserting that one religion is true, it ends up asserting that all religions are false. In the Christian case, the central revelation that the fullness of God was incarnated in Jesus Christ is simply disallowed. It is the same with other faiths, especially those that are based on an objective revelation of God's will in human history. Try telling a devout Muslim that Mohammed and the Buddha are really the same. The Muslim will not encounter this as tolerant, but as exceedingly arrogant and dismissive of his or her most cherished beliefs, principal among which is the conviction that Allah is God and Mohammed is his prophet.

Thus, the concept "religion" continues to be an instrument of imperialism, despite the fact that we no longer call other people "primitive" and "heathen." Now it is used to relativize beliefs and practices that are not compatible with Western liberal capitalism. Caesar and Mammon are jealous gods. The political and economic system that we spread across the globe with evangelical zeal demands that religion be sequestered from political and economic life, and our claims of superiority over other cultures are based on our success in relativizing religious belief. "Come on," we say to the Muslims, "lighten up; don't take your beliefs so seriously. There are a lot of religions out there in the marketplace. Who's to say that yours is the only true one? Be like us. We have learned to take our Christianity with a grain of salt, to keep it private and not take its claims too seriously in public. We have learned that the marketplace has many different religions to sell, and that each consumer ought to choose his or her own without interference. Live and let live. *And if you don't agree with us about this, you are clearly irrational and fanatical, and we reserve the right to bomb the hell out of you.*"

God against Religion

Today there rages in universities a debate among anthropologists and religious studies scholars over whether or not the term "religion" should be dropped. Arguments for dropping "religion" point to various issues: In the West, the concept came into existence only since the fifteenth century, and non-European cultures had no such concept until we gave it to them. Scholars are not even close to settling on a definition of religion, and as a consequence, all sorts of beliefs and practices, from belief in one God to belief in many gods to belief in no gods at all, are lumped together as religions. In various scholarly texts, the range of things treated as religious includes Japanese tea ceremonies, Marxism, nationalism, witchcraft, cults of ancestors, cults of celebrities (e.g., Elvis or Princess Diana), and sports (e.g., baseball or NASCAR racing). The term has been used in such a confused fashion that it seems practically useless to some.[28] So why has the term persisted nonetheless?

Because the term has been useful for certain vested interests. The term "religious" is used along with its twin "secular" to mark out two distinct spaces, one prone to irrationality and subjectiveness, and therefore best kept private, the other rational, universal, and public. As we have seen, the term "religion" has accompanied the domestication of Christianity. It has facilitated the marginalization of the radical claims of the gospel and the transfer of the Christian's ultimate loyalty to the supposedly rational spheres of nation and the market. The church is now a leisure activity; the state and the market are the only things worth dying for. The modern concept of religion facilitates idolatry, the replacement of the living God with Caesar and Mammon.

But God is not religious. Religion in the modern sense can be seen as an attempt to avoid God. To be more precise, religion is an attempt to mitigate the demands of revelation upon us. As we have seen, religion has become interior and private. It did this by relativizing revelation, making it one of a class of phenomena limited by our human ability to receive it. In effect, religion brings God down to the confines of the human self. For this reason, Karl Barth believed that Ludwig Feuerbach was right about religion: it is just the projection of human wants and needs onto an imaginary god. Ludwig Feuerbach was the great anti-theologian of the nineteenth century, a philosopher who believed that he had exposed the truth beneath all the fictions perpetrated by religion: "God" is not real, but just a mythical expression of our deepest desires. For Feuerbach, "God" was nothing more than the personification of the desire of the human heart for a perfect love. The resurrection of Christ was simply the expression of human longing for the certainty of continued personal existence after death. Eucharist was the highest self-enjoyment of human subjectivity. Barth wrote that the only way to refute Feuerbach was to admit that he was right about religion; in our relation to God we remain liars, always tempted to substitute our own desires, our own subjectivity, for the objectivity of God. This is the problem with the interiorization of religion. "Whoever is concerned with the spirit, the heart, and conscience, and the inwardness of man must be confronted with the question of whether he is really concerned with God and not with the apotheosis of man."[29] Barth and Feuerbach agree that to believe in religion is to believe in humanity. The difference is that Feuerbach believes in humanity while Barth believes in God.[30]

According to Barth, it is precisely as a religion that Christianity becomes a species of unbelief, for religion can be defined as "man's attempts to justify and to sanctify himself before a capricious and arbitrary picture of God."[31] Religion is just another attempt to deny what we know only through revelation: that humankind is fallen and incapable of saving itself.[32] Religion acknowledges a need for God, as in Schleiermacher's feeling of dependence, but as Barth says this need is not a "strictly needy need," because the religious person is always confident of his or her ability to satisfy the need. Faith, by contrast, grows from the real need of one who does not find God readily at hand, but rather finds himself or herself thrown back entirely on the revelation of God, a revelation that cannot be simply anticipated.[33] The religious attitude is ill-suited for receiving revelation, because it tries to grasp God for itself. In faith, as Barth says, we receive a gift. In religion we try to take it for ourselves.[34] Revelation, therefore, does not fit seamlessly into a preexisting religious framework, but rather negates religion.

What would it mean in our contemporary context to allow revelation to negate religion? Let us take the example of war. Our usual response to Jesus' commands is to fit them into a preexisting framework of privatized religion. Jesus' admonitions in the Sermon on the Mount to turn the other cheek, love your enemies, and bless those who persecute you are often taken to refer either to relationships among individuals alone or to the attitude that one takes in one's heart. It becomes possible to love one's enemies in one's heart while blowing their limbs off with cluster bombs. Because the public/private split has been enshrined by religion, a whole crucial area of human concern—that of war and peace—has been cordoned off from the radically destabilizing influence of Jesus Christ. A recent survey by the Pew Foundation reported that, even among regular churchgoers in America, only 17 percent named their faith as the primary influence on their views about the latest war against Iraq. Despite the overwhelming rejection of the war by church leaders, both Protestant and Catholic, most people were content to obey the president of the secular state and condone the killing of whomever he deemed it necessary to kill. God's Word is ignored, quarantined, or domesticated to allow us to serve other gods.

To allow revelation to resist religion would mean allowing the revelation of God in the words and work of Jesus Christ to have a direct effect on the whole of life, including politics and war. The admonitions of Jesus in the Sermon on the Mount, as Barth says, "declare the simple command of God which is valid for all men in its basic and primary sense, and which is thus to be kept until further notice."[35] The cross of Christ did not simply effect the coming of faith to the sincere heart; Christ's death at the hands of others abolished death. Barth asks, in reference to the cross, "From this standpoint, can we still speak of the justifiable killing of one man by another? Can there be any necessary or commanded extinction of human life? What would be its purpose now that by the extinction of this one human life that which is necessary and right for all has already taken place?"[36] Barth allows for the possibility of Christian participation in war, but only as an exception, one more difficult to justify than exceptions to the ban on suicide or abortion.[37] Barth believed that the Christian must always question the necessity for war and be prepared to be a conscientious objector to any war undertaken for mere human purposes.[38] In our context, then, the triumph of revelation over religion would consist, at the very least, in the refusal of Christians to abdicate discernment on the issue of war to the leaders of the secular state.

The modern concept of religion is an attempt to carve out two distinct spaces, the religious and the secular, and to banish God from the latter and domesticate God within the former. Religion attempts to limit the range of the living God, but the vacuum left does not remain empty; Caesar and Mammon come to fill the void. Although religion as we know it is a modern phenomenon, it represents a temptation to idolatry and self-assertion that is as old as Adam and Eve. To resist religion, the church must become simultaneously more humble and more bold. It must humble itself before the sheer objectivity of God in Word and sacrament and allow God to destroy the idolatries we have constructed out of our own wants. At the same time, the church must boldly proclaim the sovereignty of God over all creation and refuse to privatize the gospel. The church should carve out spaces of political truth-telling and economic sharing that resist the twin idolatries of state and market. The end of religion is not secularization. It is a renewed confidence that our God is Lord of all.

6

GOD IS ONE, HOLY, CATHOLIC, AND APOSTOLIC

D. Brent Laytham

For five chapters we've told you what God is not: nice, American, capitalist, religious, passively present or inexplicably absent. Now I will seek to turn the corner and say who God is. Of course, along the way we've already made several significant claims about who God is. For example, Steve Long concluded his essay by saying that ". . . God is love and God is kind and God is, in God's own self, gift and reception, the fullness of life." Such claims require both care and courage, but they must be made because the church of Jesus Christ is not called to silence, but to speak and sing and live God's praise.

This chapter develops in three parts. First, I seek to say more clearly why and how we engage in the exceedingly complex task of saying who God is. Thomas Aquinas's understanding of analogy helps us say neither too little nor too much. Second, I examine our cultural context in light of the first three commandments of the Decalogue. I suggest that keeping these commandments is absolutely essential for telling the truth about God, yet exceedingly difficult in our present moment. This leads directly to the final section, which affirms that the church is called to be one, holy, catholic, and apostolic precisely because God is one, holy, catholic, and apostolic. As Christ made God visible in the world, so the church continues his mission of showing the world the living God.

Why and How We Say "God Is . . ."

If God is truly who Christians say, then speaking of God will never be a simple matter. This is because most of our speech is about things that are part of this world. Yet God is not part of the world, but the world's Creator, so we cannot speak about God carelessly. But we can and must speak about God. There are two key reasons for this, and they are integrally related. First, we can speak truly about God because God has been, and remains, the first and primary speaker in the conversation. Second, we can speak truly about God because our speech participates in the ongoing conversation of the Son and Spirit with the Father.

I call this first reason "speaking after." For Christians, it could never suffice to claim that God is beyond our words. We can speak of God not because of the power of our intellect or the capacity of our speech, but because God has already spoken. Central to the story of Israel is the God who speaks in creation—"Then God said . . ." (Gen. 1:3), in covenant—"Now the Lord said . . ." (Gen. 12:1), and in commandment—"Then God spoke all these words" (Exod. 20:1). A central claim in Jesus' story is that the *Word* of God lived among us (John 1:14), that in him God "has spoken to us" (Heb. 1:2). Apart from what God has done, speaking of God would be impossible: "no one has ever seen God" (John 1:18a). But because "God's only Son . . . has made [God] known" (John 1:18b), speaking of God is not only possible, it is necessary: "We cannot keep from speaking about what we have seen and heard," said Peter and John after being ordered to keep silent (Acts 4:20). In other words, in the scriptural story God's "I am" precedes every claim that "God is" or that "God is not."[1] God's own revelation brings into speech a knowledge of God that requires an ongoing chain of witness. This is always a speaking after, a second word prompted and informed by God's first. The character of Scripture is not a *seeking* after—a human quest for God, but a *speaking* after—a repetition of divine speech and action that calls us into question.

There is a second reason we can speak about God. It is because in our speech about God we do not speak in isolation and in our own strength. I suggest that "speaking with" gets at the trinitarian character of our knowledge of and speech about God. We know God through the Son and the Spirit.[2] Likewise, we speak about God through the Son and in the Spirit. If we know God, it is by virtue of what God has said and done in the person of the Son, and what God has shown and shared in the person of the Spirit. Likewise, if we speak truly of God, it is by virtue of God speaking in the Son and sharing in the Spirit. Thus John's claim that we worship God "in spirit and in truth" (John 4:24) is best read as a claim that our God-talk occurs in the Holy Spirit and in Jesus who is God's truth. Paul suggests in two separate passages that we join with Jesus the Son in addressing the Father by the power of the Holy Spirit (Rom. 8:14–16; Gal. 4:6). We speak of God through the Son and in the power of the Holy Spirit.[3]

Knowing that we "speak after" and "speak with" God is not the whole story, however. We still need to consider how the predicates work in sentences that begin with "God is." For example, in this book's introduction, I alluded to a childhood table grace: "God is great. God is good. Let us thank God for this food." What do we mean when we say "good" or "great" in relation to God? Obviously, we do not mean that God is good in the way that we might say "it would be good if the Cubs won the World Series"—as good as that would be! Nor do we mean by "God is great" the same things we mean when we say that "lowfat yogurt is great" or "Streep is a great actress" or "sex is great" or even "Mother Teresa is (or was) great." But this last example suggests that there may be some relationship in the way we use the word for God and the way we use it elsewhere, for we believe that Mother Teresa's greatness is related somehow to God's.

To get at the relationship, we need to turn to Thomas Aquinas for assistance.[4] He offers a sophisticated account of theological language which suggests that much (though not all) of our speech about God is analogical. Understanding how analogical language works will protect us from expecting too much or too little from our God-talk. We expect too much if we assume that "God is good" and "cookies are good" both use the word "good" in precisely the same way. That view sees theological language as *univocal*—the word means exactly the same thing in both sentences. It mistakes God for just another thing in the world (rather than being Creator of the world), and assumes that our language for God can fully capture or comprehend God. But because God will always be more than we can fully understand, we may say something about God that is true—like "God is good"—without fully understanding what "good" means in our statement.

We expect too little if we assume that "God is love" and "Christians must love" both use the word "love" in a completely unrelated way. That view sees theological language as *equivocal*—either there is no relation between the two uses of the word or the relationship is impossible to discover. It mistakes God for someone absent who has no relation to our attempt to use language to refer truly to God. But God has an ongoing relation with us as the Creator, which means that our creaturely language has some meaningful relationship when used of God and of something in creation.

In sum, according to Aquinas, our words for God are neither *univocal* nor *equivocal*. When we speak truly of God we are neither capturing God in language nor saying nothing at all. Instead, we are using language *analogically*, so that words drawn from the finite realm mean different but not entirely unrelated things when affirmed of something finite and of God.[5] There is a relationship between the use of the word for God and its use for some thing. For example, take the word "good." First of all, if anything is good, it will be because God is the cause or source of all goodness (see Matt. 10:18). Second, no finite thing can ever embody what "good" means in the same way that God does. Third, the full definition of what "good" truly means will come from God, not from other things that we call good. That is to say, though we get to know a word like "good" through its use to describe many things that are not God, the true and primary source of the definition of "good" is God. We are called to "get to know" the full and true meaning of such words by getting to know God.

In other words, because we use language for God analogically, we are called into a process of interpretation where we grow in our knowledge of what the words mean precisely by growing in our knowledge of the one to whom the words refer. We get to know what the words do and do not mean as we get to know God. For example, to call God "the living God" is to use the word "living" to say more and mean more than we fully know; it certainly says and means more than it does when used of a person. "Living God" does mean that God is the source of all life. But it doesn't mean that God is a carbon-based life-form (as is every other living thing that we know). And it doesn't mean that God has a body (as do other living creatures). Because God is God, it will be God who defines precisely what "living" means when applied to God, not vice versa.[6] But we will come to know that meaning only in and through coming to know God.

So if our *relationship* to God is distorted, then our God-talk will be distorted too. And contrariwise, if our *understanding* of God is messed up, our relationship to God will surely be messed up too. Another way to put the matter would be to say that violating the first commandment (about relationship to God) usually leads to violations of the second and third commandments as well (about God images and God words, respectively). And likewise, violation of the second or third commandment will certainly lead to trouble with the first. In the section which follows, I argue that these days Western Christianity has significant trouble with all three.

Knowing God and Keeping Commandments

Keeping the commandments has never been a matter of rule following; it has always been about following the God who led Israel out of Egypt and the Christ who said "I am the way" (John 14:6). The first commandment speaks directly to relationship with God, the second to images and imaginations of God, and the third to words for and about God (see Exod. 20:1–7). Getting them right has never been easy. Getting them wrong has never been easier than it is now amidst the ruins of Western Christianity.[7] As earlier essays have focused on key aspects of our present difficulties, it would be possible to expound here the way that these distort commandment keeping. For example, Bill Cavanaugh's description of Christianity's metamorphosis into a religion suggests that commandment keeping would have to be a private, inner, and relative pursuit. It would finally become little more than an individual's personal opinion about how to live. That is a far cry from God's commanding claim on the people Israel! In what follows, I want to highlight three other cultural features that make it harder for us to keep the commandments, and thereby make it harder for us to say truthfully who God is and what God is not.

The Decalogue begins by announcing a nonnegotiable: "I am the Lord your God . . ." (Exod. 20:2). Even though there were other gods to choose from, for Israel the choice had already been made: "you shall have no other gods before me" (Exod. 20:3). God chose them in election and exodus, and they bound themselves to that choice when they said, "Everything that the Lord has spoken we will do" (Exod. 19:8; see also 24:7). God's declaration and claim on Israel is not a restriction that binds, however, but an invitation to be free from false gods and false claims. The ten words that follow include every dimension of life. However it might be with other gods, to serve this God is a community-enfolding, life-encompassing, allegiance-demanding whole.[8] When Yahweh says, "I am your God," it is an invitation to the freedom of absolute allegiance.

Contrast Israel's choice for the freedom of service with contemporary culture's servitude to freedom of choice. This is nowhere more visible than in the rampant individualistic consumerism that pervades Western society. Where once consumption served individualism, now it is the other way around: consumption is the primary thing, and the individual serves it.[9] In a culture permeated by consumption, persons are individualized and socialized to be consumers; the vision of human flourishing is not serving God eternally, but serving self endlessly. This apotheosis of desire for things—in biblical terms "coveting"—has a dramatic impact on human relation to God. The commandment against coveting is, after all, tenth for a reason. It is a final exclamation point on the first commandment's claim for an allegiance to God that is undiluted and unfettered. Coveting may take different forms at different times, but it is always a turning from ultimate allegiance to and desire for God. This turning in Western capitalism is virtually without limit, as Walter Brueggemann suggests:

> The propensity to covet in our society is enacted through an *unbridled consumerism* that believes that the main activity of human life is to accumulate, use, and enjoy more and more of the available resources of the earth. An *undisciplined individualism* has taught us that we are entitled to whatever we may want no matter who else may be hurt.[10]

These cultural forces have led, according to Reginald Bibby, to fragmentation: "The gods of old have been neither abandoned nor replaced. Rather, they have been broken into pieces and offered to religious consumers in piecemeal form."[11] In Bibby's suggestive phrase, this relegates God to "an à la carte role" with "little to say about everyday life."[12] The subtlety of the shift is that God is not explicitly refused or renounced.

God-talk may remain virtually unchanged. But practices of God allegiance—what Frederick Herzog once called "godwalk"—are profoundly altered. In the à la carte role, God is no longer ruler over all of life. Now God must vie for attention, compete for attachment and allegiance—perhaps even learn to tolerate, if not other gods, at the very least rival commitments. God must prove useful or helpful or desirable on consumerist grounds. Churches are pressured and seduced to be purveyors of religious goods and services.[13] The contemporary turn to spectacle in worship, the increasing clamor for "practical preaching," the bundling of God with games and "gear" in youth ministry, these are triage for a God à la carte.[14] In a context like this, keeping the first commandment is virtually impossible. It's hard to "have no other gods before me" if we've moved God to the side of our plate.

The Decalogue continues, "you shall not make for yourself an idol" (Exod. 20:4). Most interpretations of this commandment begin with the misconception that the "idol" is a representation of one of the other gods forbidden by the first commandment. Thus, one could not break this commandment without also inherently breaking the first. Exegetically, that mistakes the point: what is forbidden is an unauthorized image of Yahweh.[15] Biblical commentators are clear that the original point of the command was that Israel not make images of Yahweh. For whoever represents God in material and tangible form thereby locates and domesticates God.[16]

For us, idolatry is less about visible images of Yahweh—what we make with our hands. Our idolatry is more about verbal imaginations of Yahweh—what we do with our speech, and about lived images of Yahweh—what we do with our bodies. But the point remains the same: *the critical danger is not an image of a false god, but a false image of the true God.* In other words, Christians are less likely to worship something that they know is not God, but are rather likely to bring the God that they do worship into the orbit of something else. This second thing becomes the center—the central imagination of reality—around which even God must meaningfully revolve.

Yet the idolatry hides itself under pious rhetoric that refuses to acknowledge the de-centering of God.

Take this example: a seminary student gave me a copy of a photograph of a church sign. The permanent portion of the sign had the name of the congregation and the words "Jesus saves." The movable portion contained this message: "Go Bush Go. Praise the Lord. Pass the ammo." In the background, a large American flag blows in the breeze. Seeing the idolatry in such a picture is not difficult. Naming it is more difficult. However certain one might be that God is neither a registered Republican nor a card-carrying member of the National Rifle Association, the distortion is not that a political party or a president or a political action committee has been deified. The distortion is rather that God is brought into the orbit of another allegiance. In consequence, God no longer binds us but is bound by us; God's freedom is prescribed by our commitments.[17] And unlike the sign in the picture, most of our idolatries are far less blatant, far more insidious.

Finally, the Decalogue commands care with the divine name: "You shall not make wrongful use of the name of the Lord your God" (Exod. 20:7). This command begins with the assumption that God's name has been given and we know it. At the burning bush God reveals the divine name Yahweh—"I am who I am" (Exod. 3:14). In crucifixion and resurrection, God reveals the divine "name that is above every name"—Jesus is Lord (Phil. 2:9–11). In baptism, Christians have, from the beginning, been incorporated into the name of the Father and Son and Holy Spirit (see Matt. 28:19–20). God has indeed shared God's name with us. This extraordinary gift calls for exquisite care; the name must never be misused.

This means, first, that "God" is not a concept, but a name. Or more accurately, we Christians should say that the name of our God is Yahweh, and Father, Son, and Holy Spirit. Second, this means that God and God's names are not our thought or our idea. God is revealed to us. Therefore, "only those who know the name of God can actually transgress" this commandment.[18] Indeed, only those who know this name and have "taken it" as a fundamental identity description can violate the commandment. Non-Christians may misuse the *word* "god," but they cannot misuse God's *name*. Christian misuse of the name will generally be not only a matter of speech but also of life.

There is a line of interpretation that presumes against the commandment's implicit claim that God's name has been given and we know it. Call it functionalism. Most simply, it assumes that all language for God is metaphorical, and that all language for God is generated by persons (rather than by God). In other words, and by way of contrast with more traditional theologies of revelation, it refuses the claim that knowledge of God and language for God is a gift from God to us.[19]

The trend to assume that all God-talk is merely metaphor is epitomized by a children's book by Sandy Eisenberg Sasso entitled *In God's Name*.[20] She begins with the story of creation as found in Genesis 2. God creates the world and a dilemma as well: everything had a name, but nobody knew God's name. Then comes Sasso's decisive move. Rather than continue to tell the biblical story, in which God reveals God's name, she says, "So each person searched for God's name" (5). And the next few pages show how each person gives God a name rooted in her or his own experience. The farmer calls God source of life (6), a girl with golden skin calls God creator of light (8), and so forth (9–11, 16–23). As Sasso tells the story, and as beautifully illustrated by Phoebe Stone, the diversity of these names for God is natural, good, and beautiful. But that diversity leads first to confusion (13) and then to conflict (13–14). The problem is that the people "tried to tell one another that their name was the best, the only name for God, and that all other names were wrong" (24). The solution comes when all the people come together around a lake. There they see reflected "their own faces and the faces of all the others" (29). They all say their names for God at the same time, and a miraculous transformation occurs: "At that moment, the people knew that all the names for God were good, and no name was better than another" (31). Twice Sasso tells us that when persons claimed that their name was best, "no one listened. *Least of all, God*" (14, 24). This sets the stage for the ending's dramatic reversal, for when each offers their name for God without competition (29) and then all together unite voices to call God "one" (31), Sasso writes, "Everyone listened. Most of all, God" (32).

In God's Name is a winsome book. It affirms the goodness of an inclusive human community. It celebrates the gift of human diversity. It affirms God's desire for peace. But these qualities should not obscure the fundamentally modern and liberal story that the book tells.[21] That story goes like this: human well-being depends on liberation from the false notion of God's involvement in the world and from excessive allegiance to particular ways of belonging to God. Human well-being is accomplished by humans alone (though perhaps with God's approval). In Sasso's story, and in much of modernity, "after God created the world" (5) God did and does nothing but listen! God neither calls nor gives nor speaks nor saves. In the liberal story, claims that God speaks from cloud and fire, claims that "God was in Christ," claims that God raised Jesus from the dead and poured out the Spirit on gathered disciples, are mistaken and dangerous.

This refusal of the active and loquacious God of Israel is often buttressed by a theory about how religious language works. It begins with the claim that God's transcendence (God's existence beyond our control) puts God beyond the capacity of language. So when we speak of God, we speak metaphorically—drawing language from our own experience and applying it to God. Sasso's book obviously thinks about religious language in this way, and so does a good bit of contemporary theology. According to this approach, to think that our language about God says anything *about God* is always a theological mistake, because God-talk can never be anything more than metaphor. And metaphor is finally equivocal language, not analogical or univocal.

Ironically, this position is regularly justified by appeal to Thomas Aquinas. The confusion begins when Aquinas's careful articulation of analogy is taken to be the same thing as metaphor.[22] For example, Catherine LaCugna suggests that for Aquinas "all biblical names and forms of address to God are metaphors."[23] This claim all too easily shifts from the view that our language inadequately but truly names God because God makes it capable of more, to the view that language is inadequate to name God so our use of language to name God is always a metaphorical projection from our experience. There is a subtle turn from reception to projection. "Analogy" suggests language capacitated by God. "Metaphor" suggests language expressive of humanity's aspirations toward or experience of God. Sasso's book for children epitomizes the message of much contemporary theology: all God-talk is humanly produced, humanly projected metaphor. Speech is not capable of God, and to think otherwise makes you part of the problem rather than the solution.

This last point leads to a further shift. If all God-talk is metaphor, and if misusing or misunderstanding this leads to significant social and political ills, then why not use God-talk to make the world a better place? If "it's all metaphor" anyway, then why not choose a metaphor that fits our agenda? That is to say, if God is finally ineffable, so that our metaphors for God cannot be judged by how well or poorly they refer to God, then let's evaluate them by how useful they are for our projects and concerns. That describes theological functionalism in a nutshell: it looks for metaphors that suit its own purposes.[24] William Placher says that ". . . the attraction [of theological functionalism] is easy to understand. Most of us have causes we believe in with some passion. We would like to think that God is on our side. It is therefore tempting if we are told that we can design God to fit our specifications."[25] The irony is that under the guise of keeping the second and third commandments, God's name is refused and "a worse form of idolatry, of bringing the divine under our control," is enacted.[26] Placher concludes his critique of functionalism by affirming the necessity of reception: "We have to try to hear God speak to us, if we are to escape worshiping an idol."[27] We must stand again with Israel at the foot of Mount Sinai, trembling before smoke and fire, willing to listen as God speaks.

The One, Holy, Catholic, and Apostolic God

Placher is right to suggest that the issue is worship—not whether we will worship, but what and how.[28] A book filled with claims that "God is not" intends finally to purify praise and prayer and practice, for it is the life of Christians gathered as the church that makes it possible to say and show who God is and what God is not. These essays may make their contribution, but their point is to emphasize the necessity of the "one church under God" that Mike Baxter affirms; to call forth the church that risks the kingdom economics of the Sermon on the Mount, as Mike Budde urges; to engage the practice of discernment in the concrete community of conviction, as Rodney Clapp suggests. Only such a church can make visible the God we have named in these essays.

For too long, Christians have settled for the idea that the real church can't be seen. It is invisible, known now only to God but due to be revealed to the rest of us on the last day. Yet we should no more believe in such an invisible church than the first disciples believed in an invisible Christ. The very purpose of the church is to be a vision of who God is and what God is not. So if these essays finally fail to persuade, it may be due to our lack of critical thought or rhetorical skill. But it may also be due to the failure of the church to embody the truth that God is not American. It may be due to the failure of the church to live the kindness of God (settling instead for a conspiracy of niceness). It may be due to the church's captivity to capitalism, unable or unwilling to imagine the abundance of God's economy. It may be due to the church's willingness to sell its soul to spirituality, or to settle for being religious, rather than to embody a binding allegiance of all things to God. It may be because the church is simply lost in the crowd, competing for attention in the marketplace of desire. Where the church fails to embody truly what God is, the world is left to believe in various not-gods.

To clarify this point, I will argue that the church is called to be visibly one, holy, catholic, and apostolic precisely because God is one, holy, catholic, and apostolic. In other words, I

take these four "marks" of the church that are professed in the
Nicene Creed as being the church's true calling and authentic
character precisely because they are first God's true character.[29]
While I acknowledge from the outset the church's manifold
failures to be one, holy, catholic, and apostolic, I will not
focus on those failures; that would be a book in its own right.
Instead, I will note specific *practices* by which God's own character "marks" the identity of the church, and conclude with
the story of a church which made the one, holy, catholic, and
apostolic God visible in its own place and time.

First, God is one. Israel's thrice-daily confession, the Shema,
puts it this way: "Hear O Israel, the Lord your God, the Lord is
one" (Deut. 6:4). Christian faith, likewise, affirms that there is
"one God and Father of all, who is above all and through all and
in all" (Eph. 4:6; see also Rom. 3:30, 1 Cor. 8:6, and 1 Tim. 2:5).
Indeed, "One of the most dominant themes throughout the
Bible is the declaration of the oneness of God."[30] This central
claim that God is one requires careful reflection; we must not
assume that the one God is solitary, isolated, or obvious.

God is not solitary, because God is Triune. That is to say,
the one God is Father, Son, and Holy Spirit, three persons who
are eternally the one God. God's unity is—and has been from
all eternity—the unity of Father, Son, and Holy Spirit. Normally, we think of something that is "one" as being singular
rather than social. Such calculation will not do for a Christian
understanding of God, however. The doctrine of the Trinity
does not treat God as an arithmetic problem to be solved, but
rather seeks to unpack the full meaning of Jesus' saying "I and
the Father are one." That oneness is not an identity, as when
we discover that Peter Parker and Spiderman are actually one
and the same. It is instead a unity of relation, of nature, and
of action.

Rather than unpack the way in which theologians talk about
the unity of the three divine persons, I want to emphasize the
difference that it makes. If the one God is Triune, then there
are relationships that are internal to the divine life: the Father
related to the Son and the Holy Spirit, the Spirit to the Son and
the Father, and so forth. This means that God is not like a cue

ball in pool, which is able to relate to the other balls only on the surface, only outside the center of its own existence. A cue ball has only external relations; indeed, to get inside a cue ball is to destroy it. God is not like a cue ball because, first, God has relations that are internal to God. The Triune relations of the Father, Son, and Holy Spirit are internal to God in such a way that they neither divide nor destroy God, but are the very basis of God's existence. God is not like a cue ball because, second, God graciously chooses to relate to creation by inviting and initiating a participation in God's internal relationship. Some people think that God relates to the world or to people a lot like a cue ball—randomly knocking them around the pool table of life, drilling them into the side pocket whether they're ready to go or not—but that mistakes the oneness of God for a singularity. Because God's oneness is a Triune relation, we are invited to enter into God's own life.

Yet both the claim that there is one God and the invitation to enter into God's life are contested; the one God is not obvious. Regardless of how much Christians have come to take it for granted, the existence and identity of the one God is not something that "everybody just knows." Indeed, taking for granted the obviousness of the one God is the path to God à la carte, to lives claimed by multiple allegiances to various unrecognized gods. If we or the world are to truly see that God is one, it will be in and through a life in which allegiance is so radical, so total, that we can only describe it as *one*. Christians claim that such a unitary allegiance was made visible in Jesus. The absolute devotion of his life—embodied by the prayer in Gethsemane "not my will but thy will be done"—fulfills the first commandment as it both witnesses to the one God and denies every other god.[31]

Both Israel and the church have been called to manifest this same allegiance in their common life. We are to make the one God visible first to ourselves and then to the rest of the world. In the church, there are various practices that embody the oneness of God. A central practice is baptism, which is directly related to the oneness of God in Ephesians 4:5: "There is . . . one Lord, one faith, one baptism, one God and Father. . . ."

Perhaps the most common practice of God's oneness is not the baptism itself, but the weekly gathering of the baptized for worship on the Lord's Day. I want to focus briefly on the way the gathering of the baptized for worship is an enactment of the oneness of God.

First, it enacts the *totality of allegiance* that the living God requires over against every other divine pretender. A god is what we worship. Gathering to worship the Triune God says that this god rules our time by shaping it around weekly worship. And (even if only for an hour) it says "no" to the attempts of other gods—sport, entertainment, work, school—to rule our days. Gathering to worship the Triune God says that this god rules our bodies by calling them to a particular place and activity. It says "no" to the idea that the dominion of the one God is just an idea that we think or believe in our heads, without consequences for our bodies.

Next, assembling together as the community of the baptized forms a *visibly united people* whose unity proclaims the oneness of God. The assembly of the baptized must refuse to recognize the validity of the divisions that structure our world. For the baptized assembly, there is neither Jew nor Greek, slave nor free, male nor female (see Gal. 3:27–28). For the baptized assembly, there is neither American nor Iraqi, neither black nor white, neither "respectable folk" nor "riffraff." To continue to recognize these distinctions would be to say that they are basic to who we are, more basic even than our baptism. To gather as the church in ways that recognize or embody or reinforce these distinctions would be to acknowledge the existence of other gods. If nation or race or class condition our baptismal identity, then God is not one; rather, there would be many gods, each owning or ruling a piece of us.

Finally, gathering as the baptized acknowledges that our salvation is *participation in the Triune life of the one God*. Because God is social rather than singular, our salvation is an entrance into the community of the divine life. Assembling for worship embodies God's communal life precisely in a way that suggests that our salvation is an entrance into and participation in the divine life, the community of the Son with the Father through the Spirit. It reminds us continually that we are one, not because we have made the effort or chosen to be, but because we have been given the gift of participation in God's own unity. The practice of assembly enacts a visible unity that is analogous to God's unity precisely as, and only because, it is a participation in the oneness of the Triune God.

Second, God is holy. "Holy, holy, holy" proclaim the seraphim that circle the heavenly throne in Isaiah's vision (Isa. 6:3). The four living creatures in John's vision circle the throne of God, singing ceaselessly, "Holy, holy, holy, the Lord God the Almighty, who was and is and is to come" (Rev. 4:8). "Holy, holy, holy Lord, God of power and might" the church has sung for a millennium and a half in the Eucharist. Defining God's holiness is tricky business, since one could all too easily seek to capture God by a concept. One of my theological dictionaries gets the definition of "holy" just right by giving a cross-reference rather than a definition: "holy—see God." To call God holy is to affirm God's glory and majesty; our proper response is worship and praise. To call God holy is to affirm God's absolute goodness and radical purity; our proper response is confession and repentance (see Isa. 6:5). To call God holy is to acknowledge that God is God and we are not; our proper response is to take great care that we do not confuse our projects and perceptions with God, that we do not presume to manipulate or manage God for our mutual gain, that we do not commit the sacrilege of saying "God and . . . ," which inevitably draws God into the orbit of our own ideologies and commitments.

If "holy—see God" gets the source and center of holiness exactly right, it does not tell the full story. The holy God of the scriptural story has continually called for and called forth a holy people. "You shall therefore be holy, for I am holy" (Lev. 11:45), God said to Israel. Or "Christ loved the church and gave himself up for her, in order to make her holy . . ." (Eph. 5:25b–26a). The New Testament imagery for the church—holy priesthood, holy nation, holy temple, saints—suggests that belonging to God means being claimed to make God's holiness visible in the world. The theological dictionary needs to say also "holy—see church." Of course, any claim that the church makes visible the meaning of "holy" is bound to elicit reactions from incredulity to hostility. The church's media image these days is anything but holy: sex scandals, bitter ideological struggles, petty politics, and financial scams are regular fare. These ugly realities are evidence of how far the church has failed to embody the beauty of holiness, yet they do not completely preclude the possibility that by grace the church participates in God's own holiness in ways that grasp and transform us.

There are specific practices of the holiness of God by which the church participates in and with the holy God. First, note the way that time is sanctified—claimed for God and for God's purpose—by the commandment to "remember the Sabbath, and keep it holy" (Exod. 20:8). When Christians moved their gathering day to Sunday, they made clear that the motive was still a remembering that makes holy. They called it "Lord's Day" in witness to the risen Lord whose reign their gathering proclaimed. Thus the primary locus for the revelation of the holy God is not place or space; ostensibly Christians can gather to worship God anywhere. The primary locus that reveals God's holiness is what happens in time—the events of Exodus and Jesus' life, death, and resurrection, and the ongoing remembrance of these events in ritual repetition in Jewish or Christian worship. In a culture that makes time a commodity to vend ("spending time") or hoard ("saving time"), the Christian practice of keeping the Lord's Day holy witnesses to a God who gifts us with the time to become holy as God is holy. Thus my claim has nothing to do with nostalgia for blue laws (legislation that prevented various forms of commerce on Sundays) and everything to do with anticipation of the completion of God's work in us. "Finish then thy new creation, pure and spotless let us be," penned Charles Wesley. The practice of Lord's Day worship, and concomitant practices of sanctifying the entire day, are a public political witness to the one God who is holy, holy, holy.[32]

Third, God is catholic. We tend to think of catholicity as a spatial claim, implying universal or all-encompassing extension. A good synonym might be "global." There are dangers in thinking about God as catholic in this sense, for it can too easily diminish God's glory or restrict God's freedom. Nevertheless, to speak of God as catholic in a global sense is helpful to the degree that it forbids the kind of idolatry that Mike Baxter described in "God Is Not American." God is no respecter of the divisions that we create and defend; God is not here-but-not-there, or with-us-against-them.

I want to suggest a deeper understanding of God's catholicity, rooted in the word's original meaning of "according to the whole." This implies first a wholeness, completeness, or fullness. God is catholic in the sense that God is fully sufficient, lacking nothing, super-abundantly rich. God's excessive fullness is not static either, but an ever-flowing and overflowing sharing of life and love among the Father, Son, and Holy Spirit. Second, "according to the whole" implies that this divine fullness is fully present in each of the three divine persons: the Father is entirely God, the Son is completely God, the Holy Spirit is wholly God. Each one is fully the fullness of God. They are not parts of God nor partially God, but each one is fully and completely God in a way that does not exclude or divide but invites and relates.

Jesus Christ reveals both dimensions of this divine catholicity, for "in him all the fullness of God was pleased to dwell" (Col. 1:19; see Eph. 4:10). In a strange paradox, we see the excessive fullness of God in one who emptied himself (Phil. 2:7), in one who died in order to draw all people into the fullness of divine life (John 12:32). Thus catholicity means Jesus Christ. We call the church catholic, not first because of a geographical extension through space or a historical extension through time, but because of its foundation by and relationship to Jesus Christ, "him who fills all in all" (Eph. 1:23). Ignatius of Antioch pointed to this christological center of catholicity when he said, "Wherever Jesus Christ is, there is the catholic church" (Smyrneans 8:2). We need only to add, wherever Jesus Christ is, there is the catholic God.

Without a doubt, the central practice of God's catholicity is the Eucharist (or Lord's Supper or Holy Communion). For it is the sacrament of the fullness of the presence of Jesus Christ. In it, the fullness of divine life is offered as feast. In it, the wholeness of human community in God, indeed the completion of creation in Christ, is anticipated as feast. The Eucharist thus claims the church for God's own brand of catholicity. Every human exclusion and division is meant to be judged by the catholicity of Christ's communion table. But it does not create an undifferentiated uniformity, the mass culture of the crowd (see Rodney Clapp's chapter). Rather, the eucharistic table creates a unity in difference and variety, a community that welcomes diversity by incorporating it into the fullness of Christ.

Fourth, God is apostolic. An apostle is one who is sent on a mission or with a message. God is just such a sending God, as every child who has memorized John 3:16 knows. For God sent the Son into the world in order that the world might be saved (John 3:17). As the sent one, Jesus is described as being appointed "the apostle" (Heb. 3:1). Moreover, Jesus has sent the Holy Spirit on and in the church (John 20:22; Luke 24:49; Acts 2:33; Gal. 4:6). Thus the Father sends and the Son and Spirit are sent; God is apostolic.

The church is apostolic because it participates in this mission of the Father sending the Son and the Spirit. Following his resurrection, Jesus told the disciples, "As the Father has sent me, so I send you" (John 20:21). Representatives of the church are "sent out by the Holy Spirit" (Acts 13:4). The Great Commission is best read as a sending of the whole church into the world to make disciples (Matt. 28:16–20). Thus, the whole church participates in God's apostolicity. And the adjective "apostolic" is best seen as first and primarily a description of the church's relation to God in Jesus Christ, not as a description of particular individuals.

Rather than highlight a specific practice of apostolicity, it seems best to affirm that the entire life of the church—in all of its varied practices—is meant to embody participation in the Father's sending of the Son and Spirit for the sake of the world. To do that, I turn to the story of a church whose common life and shared practice makes visible, albeit imperfectly, the God who is apostolic, catholic, holy, and one.

The connection that I am suggesting between the practice of church and the doctrine of God is nicely illustrated by the story of Our Lady of Guadalupe Catholic Church in Newton Grove, North Carolina. When I first drove up to Our Lady of Guadalupe in 1997, the church sign caught my eye. "Welcoming all people since 1874," it said. "Yeah, right," I thought, "more likely you've been welcoming all 'our kind of people' since 1874." Given the history of race relations in the sandhills of North Carolina, I was skeptical that even a church could have resisted racial exclusions for more than 100 years. I had come to expect the church at worship to look more like a mirror of social exclusions than like a window on kingdom embrace. In the case of Our Lady of Gaudalupe, however, I was profoundly wrong.

Our Lady of Guadalupe's story began with a Methodist physician named John Carr Monk. In the years following the Civil War, Monk was greatly disturbed when his local Methodist church resolved to exclude African Americans. Monk began to pray about a church where blacks and whites would worship together as children of the one God, as brothers and sisters of the same Christ. During that time, he read a newspaper article in which Archbishop of New York John McCloskey expounded the "marks of the church" as professed in the Nicene Creed. Monk was persuaded that just such a church was needed in Newton Grove, for he was convinced that a "one, holy, catholic, and apostolic church" would surely get race relations right. He wrote a letter of inquiry addressed simply to "any Catholic priest" in Wilmington, North Carolina. And the rest (as they say) is history, the beautiful and human history of a Christian congregation "welcoming all people since 1874." Priests came to give instruction in the Christian faith, a church was organized, a building built, and a congregation grew—a congregation in which the dividing wall of hostility (Eph. 2:14) between white and black was broken down.

When I visited, more than a century later, I found a church that was bilingual, multiracial, and multiethnic, a church that led its community in servant ministry to the poor, a church that had for more than fifteen years been working hard at ecumenical conversation about Christian unity with the various other denominations in Newton Grove. In short, I was introduced to a church that embodied "what God is not." Our Lady of Guadalupe is a living witness that God is not divided—by race, by class, by language; that God is not insular—but giving and loving and serving. It is this only because it corporately practices and visibly enacts the reality that God is—one, holy, catholic, and apostolic. John Carr Monk's prayer, which is only a repetition of the high priestly prayer of Jesus Christ (John 17), continues to be answered. That is finally the hope of this book: that readers will inhabit congregations where attention to what God is not will lead to more faithful embodiment of all that God is.

Notes

Introduction

1. At times, one could do far worse than join Job in silence and repentance. "Then Job answered the Lord: 'See, I am of small account; what shall I answer you? I lay my hand on my mouth. I have spoken once, and I will not answer; twice, but will proceed no further'" (Job 40:3–5). ". . . I despise myself, and repent in dust and ashes" (Job 42:6).

2. See his *Summa Theologica*, preface to question 13.

3. Throughout I will speak of Christian conviction rather than Christian belief. This is primarily because we Christians have become far too comfortable with beliefs that demand nothing from us. Phyllis Tickle notes that "one of the defining characteristics of the religious experience in this country [the United States], as it is observed and reported by those of other nationalities, is our near complete separation of belief from action." Phyllis Tickle, *God-Talk in America* (New York: Crossroad, 1997), 177 note 1.

4. Stanley Hauerwas, *After Christendom: How the Church Is to Behave If Freedom, Justice, and a Christian Nation Are Bad Ideas* (Nashville: Abingdon, 1991), 133.

5. To learn more about The Ekklesia Project, see the website www.ekklesiaproject.org or see the appendix in Stanley Hauerwas, *A Better Hope: Resources for a Church Confronting Capitalism, Democracy, and Postmodernity* (Grand Rapids: Brazos, 2000).

6. Rowan Williams, "Different Christs," in *A Ray of Darkness: Sermons and Reflections* (Boston: Cowley, 1995), 88.

7. Williams, "Different Christs," 89, italics original.

8. Tickle, *God-Talk in America*, 174.

9. Ibid., 175, ellipses original.

10. This is a part of the Rite of Christian Initiation of Adults of the Catholic Church. For an evangelical appropriation of baptismal exorcisms, see Robert E. Webber, *Celebrating Our Faith: Evangelism through Worship* (San Francisco: Harper and Row, 1986), 80–81.

11. As Stanley Hauerwas reminds us, "modernity and its bastard offspring postmodernity are but reflections of the Christian attempt to make God a god available without the mediation of the church." Hauerwas, *A Better Hope*, 38.

12. Quoted from the principles of The Ekklesia Project, as stated in "The Ekklesia Project: A Declaration and an Invitation to All Christians," appendix in Stanley Hauerwas and Michael L. Budde, *The Ekklesia Project: A School for Subversive Friendships* (Eugene, Ore.: Wipf and Stock, 2000), 15.

13. Stephen Arterburn and Jack Felton, *More Jesus, Less Religion: Moving from Rules to Relationship* (Colorado Springs: Waterbrook, 2000).

14. Walter Brueggemann, *Cadences of Home: Preaching among Exiles* (Louisville: Westminster John Knox, 1997), 128.

God Is Not "a Stranger on a Bus"

1. The name for the Latin translation of the Bible that was used for more than 1,500 years in Western Christianity is the "Vulgate," so named because it was originally a translation into the popular (*vulgata*) language.

2. St. Augustine, *City of God*, trans. Henry Bettenson (London and New York: Penguin, 1984), book XXII, chapter 24, 1070–76.

3. The story is found at Matthew 21:1–11, Mark 11:1–10, Luke 19:28–40, John 12:12–19.

4. Karl Barth, *Church Dogmatics* IV/1, ed. G. W. Bromiley and T. F. Torrance, trans. G. W. Bromiley (Edinburgh: T & T Clark, 1956), 427 (quoting W. Vischer).

5. Karl Barth, *Church Dogmatics* I/2, ed. G. W. Bromiley and T. F. Torrance, trans. G. T. Thomson and Harold Knight (Edinburgh: T & T Clark, 1956), 280.

6. As I argue soon in this essay, the church is called to be a convictional community of discernment in relation to popular and all other culture. I hope it is implicitly clear that this discernment entails the church's own judgment of itself. The church is not hermetically sealed off from the cultures it indwells, and it certainly is susceptible to picking up the worst elements of those cultures and then making matters worse by "baptizing" them. The Word of God in Christ, as Barth repeatedly emphasized, is never simply to be identified with the church or any of its pronouncements. The Word is never possessed by the church, but instead is the subject of which the church (and the world) is the object. Christian discernment therefore must include a keen and ongoing awareness of the human, and all too churchly, tendency to instrumentalize the Word, to subordinate revelation to religion. This was

declared with characteristic bluntness by Christoph Friedrich Blumhardt, a German pastor who greatly influenced Barth. "When it comes to what people would rather have," Blumhardt said, "whether Jesus or their own thoughts about him, they will fight to the death for their own thoughts." See Vernard Eller, ed., *Thy Kingdom Come: A Blumhardt Reader* (Grand Rapids: Eerdmans, 1980), 96.

7. Ibid., 316.

8. See James Wm. McClendon Jr. and James M. Smith, *Convictions: Defusing Religious Relativism,* rev. ed. (Valley Forge, Pa.: Trinity Press International, 1994), 150.

9. Lynda Barry cartoon, "White House Hymnal," February 26, 2003, accessed at Salon.com.

10. Barth, *Church Dogmatics* I/2, 302.

11. Ibid., 282.

12. Ibid., 291.

13. Ellen T. Charry, *By the Renewing of Your Minds* (New York and Oxford: Oxford University Press, 1997), 43 and 45.

14. See Richard J. Mouw, *When the Kings Come Marching In,* rev. ed. (Grand Rapids: Eerdmans, 2002).

15. Wendell Berry, *Sex, Economy, Freedom & Community* (New York and San Francisco: Pantheon, 1992, 1993), 147.

16. As Alasdair MacIntyre has remarked, going to war for the modern nation-state is like being asked to die for the phone company.

17. Berry, *Sex,* 148.

18. The shuttle was destroyed on February 1, 2003.

19. McClendon and Smith, *Convictions,* 5.

God Is Not Nice

1. By elaborating on these three points, I do not intend to reinstate some militaristic, patriarchal god who functions like a Marine drill sergeant. Quite the contrary, I fear that the contemporary nice god is dangerous precisely because this god does a psychological operation on us. For this reason I will argue that the sentimentality of the nice god is more patriarchal than the kind God we find presented to us by Julian of Norwich or the self-sufficient Triune God of Thomas Aquinas.

2. It may not be unrelated that the same child who thinks God is nice also thinks "God is a man."

3. See Marsha Witten's *All Is Forgiven: The Secular Message in American Protestantism* (Princeton: Princeton University Press, 1993) for a partial analysis of this trend.

4. See Walt Kallestad, *Entertainment Evangelism: Taking the Church Public* (Nashville: Abingdon, 1996).

5. Fyodor Dostoevsky, *The Brothers Karamazov,* trans. Andrew H. Mac-Andrew (Toronto: Bantam, 1981), 299.

6. We should note carefully that the Grand Inquisitor also loves the people. Moreover, he is not averse to suffering himself; he has lived the austere life of the monk.

7. Dostoevsky, *Brothers Karamazov,* 304.

8. Ibid., 305. For the Grand Inquisitor, this is not without price: "And it is in this deception that our suffering will consist, because we will have to lie!"

9. It is important to recognize that Ivan is not saying that the church does this solely for its own power and material gain. He recognizes that monks who have lived as austerely and holy as has the Grand Inquisitor do not seek material gain. The power of his story comes in the fact that the Grand Inquisitor has lost his faith in the story. He no longer wishes to serve a God who has judgment or hell. He tells the people what they want to hear so that they will be happy in this life because he fears God does not care for the sufferings of these people as much as the Grand Inquisitor himself does.

10. On the latter, see Stewart Hoover, "The Cross at Willow Creek: Seeker Religion and the Contemporary Marketplace," in *Religion and Popular Culture in America,* ed. Bruce Forbes and Jeffrey Mahan (Berkeley: University of California Press, 2000), 145–59.

11. A recent satire by Ross Werland compares Wal-Mart to church. "I was greeted, just like at church, but at church the greeter doesn't offer me a cart." "Store Aisles Laden with Sin," *Chicago Tribune,* May 25, 2003, sec. C. Not just the greeters, but the nice god of many churches welcomes us at the door with a smile and an invitation to "shop till you drop."

12. For MacIntyre's argument, see *After Virtue* (Notre Dame, Ind.: University of Notre Dame Press, 1984).

13. All quotations from Charles G. Finney, *Lectures on Revivals of Religion* (Oberlin, Ohio: E.J. Goodrich, 1868), 12, original italics removed. I am indebted to L. Edward Phillips's unpublished essay "The New and Improved Creation! The Commodification of Liturgy as Parody of a Wesleyan Theme" for bringing this passage to my attention.

14. "From its beginning, Igniting Ministry has been directed toward speaking with—not to—unchurched audiences. It was developed to provide help to those seeking spiritual fulfillment." This quote can be found at the site that explains the Igniting Ministry campaign for the United Methodist Church, www.ignitingministry.org. See especially the report entitled "2001 Findings."

15. A recent interview with Neale Donald Walsch in the *San Francisco Chronicle* shows how close the tolerant Christian niche is to the New Age spirituality niche. When asked whether he peddles "feel-good spirituality," Walsch responded, "If we can't depend on God to feel good, then why are we in this universe?" (Sunday, November 17, 2002; section E2; accessed on May

28, 2003 through LexisNexis). Methodists have yet to exploit the feel-good niche as well as Walsch; he has "sold 7 million books in 27 languages."

16. Clearly the God of the Bible is intolerant and judgmental; no rewriting of our sacred stories can escape this fact. The question is, What is it that God does not tolerate? What is it that God judges? From what are we saved?

17. See Walter Kasper, *Jesus the Christ* (London: Paulist, 1976), 22. Melanchthon writes that Christ is properly known in the doctrines of sin, the law, and grace, "for by them is Christ properly known, if indeed this is to know Christ, to wit, to know his benefits and not as they [the scholastic theologians] teach, to perceive his natures and the mode of his incarnation." Philip Melanchthon, *The Loci Communes*, ed. and trans. Charles Leander Hill (Boston: Meador, 1944), 68.

18. Kasper, *Jesus the Christ*, 22–23.

19. Woodard, "Ushering in the Age of the Laity: Some Cranky Reservations," *Commonweal* 121 (September 9, 1994): 9; quoted in Stanley Hauerwas, *Sanctify Them in the Truth: Holiness Exemplified* (Nashville: Abingdon, 1998), 235 note 2.

20. Lest the reader think I am exaggerating here, I would ask him or her to do a simple experiment. Refuse to take the Myers-Briggs personality profile, or if you've already taken it, refuse to discuss your results; refuse to answer sociological surveys. See if this does not raise eyebrows among friends and colleagues. In the contemporary church, especially if the reader seeks ordination, see if this doesn't cause more trouble than would an inability to confess or know the Nicene Creed.

21. Thomas Aquinas, *Summa Theologica* Ia 42.5, response. Father Thomas Weinandy explains it this way: "The persons of the Trinity are eternally constituted in their own singular identity only in relation to one another, and thus they subsist as who they are only within their mutual relationships. In their relationships to one another each person of the Trinity subsistently defines, and is equally subsistently defined by, the other persons. Thus the persons of the Trinity are subsistent relations." Thomas Weinandy, O.F.M., Cap., *Does God Suffer?* (Notre Dame, Ind.: University of Notre Dame Press, 2000), 116.

22. Weinandy, *Does God Suffer?* 116.

23. Aquinas says that God creates not out of need but out of love: "By affirming that there is in [God] the procession of love we show that he made creatures, not because he needed them nor because of any reason outside himself, but from love of his own goodness," Aquinas, *Summa Theologica* Ia 32.1, ad 3.

24. To have the power to rest joyfully in a divine person is ours by reason of grace alone." Aquinas, *Summa Theologica* Ia 43.3, response.

25. The date of her revelation was May 13, 1373. But it wasn't until 1393 that she wrote the long text of her revelations. The short text was written shortly after her revelation.

26. Sara Maitland, *Virtuous Magic: Women Saints and Their Meanings* (New York: Continuum, 1998), 294, quotes, "I saw God in a point and fulfilled my heart most of joy so I understood it shall be in heaven without end to all that shall come there. And he showed me a little thing the quantity of an hazelnut lying in the palm of my hand and it was as round as a ball. It is all that is made. It lasts and it ever shall last, for God loveth it and so hath all thing being by the love of God."

27. See Frederick Christian Bauerschmidt, *Julian of Norwich and the Mystical Body Politic of Christ* (Notre Dame, Ind.: University of Notre Dame Press, 1999).

28. For an excellent discussion of this, see Bauerschmidt's first chapter, "Imagining the Political," in his *Julian of Norwich.*

29. Julian of Norwich, *Revelations of Divine Love* (London: Penguin, 1998), 145.

30. She writes, "God is kind in his being: that is to say, that goodness that is kind, it is God. He is the ground, he is the substance, he is the same thing that is kindness, and he is very father and very mother of kind. And all kinds that he has made to flow out of him to work his will, shall be restored and brought again into him by the salvation of man through the working of grace." Ibid., 145.

31. Ibid., 129.

32. Bauerschmidt, "Order, Freedom and 'Kindness': Julian of Norwich on the Edge of Modernity," unpublished essay, delivered to *Lumen Christi,* University of Chicago, 1999.

33. Julian of Norwich, *Revelations,* 9.

God Is Not American

1. Mark Slouka, "A Year Later: Notes on America's Intimations of Mortality," *Harper's* 305 (September 2002): 35–43.

2. Ibid., 43.

3. Ibid., 36.

4. Ibid., 39.

5. Ibid., 37 note 1.

6. This quotation is taken from www.cnn.com/2001/US/09/14/ Falwell.apology. For a partial transcript of the broadcast in question, see www.beliefnet.com/story/87/story_8770_1.html. For an attempt to clarify the facts involved in the controversy, see www.truthorfiction.com/rumors/ falwell-robertson-wtc.htm.

7. *First Things* 118 (December 2001):11–17. In my summary and critique, I attribute this editorial to Richard John Neuhaus himself rather than "the editors" for the sake of convenience and also because it bears his distinctive prose and thought patterns. Subsequent page references to this editorial will be parenthetical.

8. Thomas Aquinas, *Summa Theologica* II/2, questions 1–6; in vol. 2, trans. Fathers of the English Dominican Province (New York: Benziger Brothers, 1947), 1169–1202.

9. Ibid., question 161.

10. *Letter to Diognetus,* in *The Apostolic Fathers,* trans. Francis X. Glimm, Joseph M.-F. Marique, S.J., and Gerald Walsh, S.J. (New York: Cima, 1947), 359. This is not the same translation as Neuhaus uses, but the differences are of no matter to the criticism I am making.

11. Ibid., 359.

12. Ibid., 359–60.

13. David Brooks, *Bobos in Paradise* (New York: Simon and Schuster, 2001).

14. Richard John Neuhaus, *The Naked Public Square* (Grand Rapids: Eerdmans, 1984).

15. He observed that history had taken a remarkable twist: Catholics, emboldened by the religious and moral vision of Pope John Paul II, were now the ones to embolden evangelical Christians and others to bring America back from the precipice and restore it to its founding religious and moral principles. Richard John Neuhaus, *The Catholic Moment* (New York: Harper and Row, 1987).

16. *First Things* 113 (May 2001): 70–73.

17. The French analyst Alexis de Tocqueville's *Democracy in America,* based on his 1832 observations and interviews, is still considered one of the most insightful and relevant studies of American life.

18. See for example Sanford Kessler, *Tocqueville's Civil Religion* (Albany: State University of New York Press, 1994).

19. "Eschatology" refers to the Christian understanding of the end of history—its purpose and goal as revealed in Jesus Christ. "Ecclesiology" refers to the doctrine of the church—its nature and purpose as revealed in Jesus Christ.

20. *Letter to Diognetus,* 360.

God Is Not a Capitalist

1. "Vatican Rescinds 'Blessed' Status of World's Meek," *The Onion,* 33: 23 (June 18, 1998). Reprinted with permission of THE ONION. Copyright 1998, by ONION, INC. www.theonion.com.

2. See Michael Budde and Robert Brimlow, *Christianity Incorporated* (Grand Rapids: Brazos, 2002).

3. Victoria Combe, "Church Plans Market Research to Gauge Views of 'Customers,'" *Daily Telegraph* (February 18, 1999).

4. Victoria Combe, "Church Puts Its Faith in TV Advertisement," *Daily Telegraph* (March 20, 1997).

5. A. J. McIllroy and Victoria Combe, "Carey Warns Church against Creating Barriers to Baptism," *Daily Telegraph* (April 14, 1997).

6. "Worship in the Fast Lane," *Daily Telegraph* (January 4, 1999).

7. Laurie Goodstein, "Archbishop-Elect Is a Man Who Takes Charge," *New York Times* (May 12, 2000).

8. Laurie Beth Jones, *Jesus CEO: Using Ancient Wisdom for Visionary Leadership* (New York: Hyperion, 1995).

9. Ibid., xi.

10. Ibid., 17 and 50–4, respectively.

11. Tom Brown, "Jesus CEO," *Industry Week* (March 6, 1995).

12. Ibid., italics original. Jones says corporations should view their employees' spirituality as an "untapped resource," insofar as at least 30 percent of each employee's potential is underutilized. Her advice is for executives to engage in spiritual techniques, "and productivity and morale will soar."

13. Ibid.

14. For Novak, see *Toward a Theology of the Corporation* (Washington, D.C.: American Enterprise Institute for Public Policy Research, 1981).

15. In Matthew 25 the standard of judgment on the last day is whatever you did for "one of the least of these" (25:40).

16. See Psalm 118:22; Mark 12:10 and parallels; Acts 4:11; 1 Peter 2: 4,7.

17. See Leviticus 25 and the discussion of it in John Howard Yoder, *The Politics of Jesus*, 2d ed. (Grand Rapids: Eerdmans, 1994), chapter 3.

18. Capitalism does, of course, have its own appreciation for bankruptcy—as a strategic matter in capitalist societies, bankruptcy is a useful way to eliminate unperforming and stagnating levels of debt, as well as a tactical way to evade pension obligations, union contracts, and liability lawsuits. But the sort of bankruptcy that God presumes and practices is a recipe for disaster according to capitalist practices.

19. For a reading of the socioeconomic context of the parable along these lines, see William R. Herzog II, *Parables as Subversive Speech: Jesus as Pedagogue of the Oppressed* (Louisville: Westminster John Knox, 1994), 150–68. Herzog's reading is helpful but inadequately christological.

20. See D. Stephen Long, *Divine Economy: Theology and the Market* (London: Routledge, 2000).

21. Cited by Marcel Dumais, "The Sermon on the Mount: An Unattainable Way of Life?" *Chicago Studies* 37:3.

22. This is a point made well by Steve Long in *Divine Economy*.

God Is Not Religious

1. Paul J. Griffiths, "The Very Idea of Religion," *First Things* 103 (May 2000): 31. The Vulgate dates from around A.D. 400, the King James from around 1611.

2. Augustine, *De Vera Religione,* 1–10, English translation in *Augustine: Earlier Writings,* trans. John H. S. Burleigh (Philadelphia: Westminster, 1953). See, for example, numbers 108–9, where Augustine compares true worship of God with false worship of human works, nature, and material things.

3. "Religion," *Oxford English Dictionary,* 2d ed. (Oxford: Clarendon, 1989).

4. Nicholas de Cusa, *De Pace Fidei,* trans. John P. Dolan in *Unity and Reform: Selected Writings of Nicholas de Cusa* (Notre Dame, Ind.: University of Notre Dame Press, 1962), 198–99.

5. Ibid., 203.

6. Wilfred Cantwell Smith, *The Meaning and End of Religion: A New Approach to the Religious Traditions of Mankind* (New York: Macmillan, 1963), 33–34.

7. Smith, *Religion,* 32–44.

8. Cherbury had a profound influence on both Grotius and René Descartes.

9. Lord Herbert of Cherbury, quoted in Graham Ward, *True Religion* (Oxford: Blackwell, 2003), 58–59.

10. On this point, see Ward, *Religion,* 91–97. In the same way, Schleiermacher would argue, the Jewish tradition allows Jews to name their "feeling of absolute dependence" God, Allah to the Muslims, and so forth.

11. One could multiply examples ranging from *The Prayer of Jabez* to *The Celestine Prophecy.*

12. Quoted in Hanna Rosin, "Believers in God, If Not Church; Many Carve Out Unique Religions," *Washington Post,* January 18, 2000, A1.

13. Rosin, "Believers in God."

14. Friedrich Schleiermacher, *On Religion: Speeches to Its Cultured Despisers,* trans. John Oman (New York: Harper and Row, 1958), 26–27.

15. John Milbank, *Theology and Social Theory: Beyond Secular Reason* (Oxford: Basil Blackwell, 1990), 9–12.

16. See John Bossy, *Christianity in the West 1400–1700* (Oxford: Oxford University Press, 1985), the first five chapters, for a summary characterization of traditional Christian society.

17. John Neville Figgis, *From Gerson to Grotius 1414–1625* (New York: Harper and Row, 1960), 5.

18. I cover a lot of this ground in my book *Theopolitical Imagination: Christian Practices of Space and Time* (Edinburgh: T & T Clark, 2003), 9–52. The privatization of the church is usually defended on the grounds that public avowals of doctrine caused much bloodshed in the sixteenth and seventeenth centuries between Catholics and Protestants. In this article I argue that these wars were fought over conflicts that far predated Luther, conflicts over the form of public authority. This explains why often Catholics fought Catholics and Protestants fought alongside Catholics in the so-called Wars of Religion.

19. Figgis, 124.

20. George F. Will, "Conduct, Coercion, Belief," *Washington Post,* April 22, 1990, B7.

21. The most influential statement of this thesis is Samuel Huntington, *The Clash of Civilizations and the Remaking of World Order* (New York: Touchstone, 1998).

22. Sister M. Juliana Bedier, *World Neighbors: Geography for the Air Age* (New York: W. H. Sadlier, 1952), 190.

23. Ibid.

24. Ibid.

25. Ibid., 192–8.

26. Russell T. McCutcheon, "The Imperial Dynamic in the Study of Religion: Neocolonial Practices in an American Discipline," in C. Richard King, ed., *Post-Colonial America* (Chicago: University of Illinois Press, 2000), 275–81.

27. See for example the volume edited by John Hick and Paul Knitter entitled *The Myth of Christian Uniqueness: Toward a Pluralistic Theology of Religions* (Maryknoll, N.Y.: Orbis, 1987).

28. The best argument for the abandonment of the category "religion" is found in Timothy Fitzgerald, *The Ideology of Religious Studies* (New York: Oxford University Press, 2000). Fitzgerald does a devastating critique of the utter incoherence of the many conflicting attempts to define religion. He also effectively dismantles the contention by some that, although religion cannot be defined, it remains a valuable concept anyway.

29. Karl Barth, "An Introductory Essay," in Ludwig Feuerbach, *The Essence of Christianity* (New York: Harper and Brothers, 1957), xxv.

30. See H. Richard Niebuhr, "Foreword," in Feuerbach, *Essence,* viii. Barth believes in humanity only insofar as the decision about humanity has been revealed once and for all in Jesus Christ. What we know about humanity comes from the revelation of God in Christ, and not from some prior examination of human nature and human subjectivity. Religion begins from human subjectivity and asks what can be known about God based on what we know of ourselves. Religion becomes, as Barth says, the "norm and principle by which to explain the revelation of God"; Karl Barth, *Church Dogmatics* I/2, ed. G. W. Bromiley and T. F. Torrance, trans. G. T. Thomson and Harold Knight (Edinburgh: T & T Clark, 1956), 284. The approach of true faith is the opposite; revelation is the norm for the interpretation of all religion. Christ is not measured by what we know of the human, but Christ becomes the standard by which the human is judged and redeemed.

31. Barth, *Dogmatics* I/2, 280.

32. Barth acknowledges that there is a proper sense in which Christianity is called a religion and placed beside the other religions of the world. Christianity as religion is not absolutely unique, but is paralleled by many of the rites and practices of other religions. Christianity is full of the same human longings for the Absolute that are found in other systems. To deny

this would be to negate revelation, for in order to be revelation, God's Word must be incarnated in the human. Nevertheless, Christianity *as* religion is unbelief (Ibid., 281–83).

33. Ibid., 315.

34. Ibid., 302. Barth nevertheless believes that we can speak of "true religion," but only and precisely as we can speak of a "justified sinner." True religion is not true in and of itself, but can only be justified from without, by the grace of God; Ibid., 325–26.

35. Barth, *Church Dogmatics* III/4, ed. G. W. Bromiley and T. F. Torrance, trans. A. T. Mackay, T. H. L. Parker, Harold Knight, Henry A. Kennedy, John Marks (Edinburgh: T & T Clark, 1961), 430.

36. Ibid., 400.

37. Ibid., 455.

38. Ibid., 456–63.

God Is One, Holy, Catholic, and Apostolic

1. See Exodus 3:14 ("I am who I am"), Exodus 20:1 ("I am the Lord your God . . ."), and Jesus' "I am" statements in the Gospel of John.

2. The Christian gospel proclaims a confident call to know God in union with Christ by the power of the Holy Spirit. "The gospel assures us that we know God as he truly is" (Colin E. Gunton, *Act and Being: Towards a Theology of the Divine Attributes* [London: SCM, 2002], 47]).

3. For an excellent elaboration of this in terms of worship, see James B. Torrance, *Worship, Community and the Triune God of Grace* (Downers Grove, Ill.: InterVarsity Press, 1996).

4. See his *Summa Theologica* Ia, 13.

5. For a carefully nuanced discussion of all this, see William C. Placher, *The Domestication of Transcendence: How Modern Thinking about God Went Wrong* (Louisville: Westminster John Knox, 1996) 28–29.

6. On this score, analogy is closer to equivocal than univocal use. Placher, in *Domestication*, writes "'Analogy' thus does not provide a neat alternative between univocity and equivocity that solves the problems. It is, Aquinas admitted, itself a type of equivocation" (31).

7. This is not to say that there are not promising possibilities in the present as well. For example, the legacy of sexism, clericalism, and Constantinianism that has burdened the church for most of its history shows some signs of being dislodged.

8. Dietrich Bonhoeffer says that other gods are tolerant, but Yahweh is not. "The First Table of the Ten Commandments," in John D. Godsey, ed., *Preface to Bonhoeffer: The Man and Two of His Shorter Writings* (Philadelphia: Fortress, 1965), 56. His point is that these other gods don't always seek to be alone; they are often willing to coexist, each making claim over a different sector of our lives.

9. Alan Storkey claims that ". . . consumption has now become the dominant faith and individualism . . . serves it." "Postmodernism Is Consumption," in Craig Bartholomew and Thorstein Moritz, *Christ and Consumerism: Critical Reflections on the Spirit of Our Age* (Carlisle: Paternoster, 2000):100–117; 100. "Consumption is the collectivist-individualist, nationalist-internationalist, the healer, the entertainer, the lover, the spiritual, the feeder and the consolation. *It is the chief rival to God in our culture*" (100, emphasis mine).

10. Walter Brueggemann, "Exodus," in Leander Keck, et al., eds., *The New Interpreter's Bible,* vol. 1 (Nashville: Abingdon, 1994), 852, emphasis mine.

11. Reginald W. Bibby, *Fragmented Gods: The Poverty and Potential of Religion in Canada* (Toronto: Irwin, 1987), 85. Though Bibby's study focuses on Canada, I am persuaded that his claims about fragmentation by consumerism are also apt for the United States.

12. Ibid., 149.

13. See Philip D. Kenneson and James L. Street, *Selling Out the Church: The Dangers of Church Marketing* (Nashville: Abingdon, 1997).

14. For a particularly odious example of such triage for a trivialized god, see Walt Kallestad, *Entertainment Evangelism: Taking the Church Public* (Nashville: Abingdon, 1996). On the dangers of spectacle, see Ralph Wood, "Hungry Eye: *The Two Towers* and the Seductiveness of Spectacle," *Books and Culture* 9.2 (March/April 2003):16–17.

15. Of course, there are authorized images of God: Jesus, who is the image of God (2 Cor. 4:4, Col. 1:15), and humans, created in or according to the image of God (Gen. 1:26).

16. Brueggemann says, "The temptation, then, is not the creation of a rival that detracts from Yahweh, but an attempt to locate and thereby domesticate Yahweh, in a visible, controlled object. . . . It does not fear a rival, but a distortion of Yahweh's free character by an attempt to locate Yahweh and so diminish something of Yahweh's terrible freedom" ("Exodus," 842).

17. I am not claiming that any of these other commitments are compatible with allegiance to God. My point here is less about the particular content of the obviously egregious example and more about the logic of idolatry.

18. Bonhoeffer, "The First Table," 61; see 60–61 for the claim that God is not our idea.

19. As both Clapp and Cavanaugh reminded us in their chapters, Karl Barth called this understanding "religion" and contrasted it with revelation.

20. Sandy Eisenberg Sasso, *In God's Name,* illustrated by Phoebe Stone (Woodstock, Vt.: Jewish Lights, 1994). Further quotes and citations will be made parenthetically.

21. See Bill Cavanaugh's chapter, "God Is Not Religious," for clarification of the modernist story that "religion" is the source of intolerance, conflict, violence, and war.

22. Placher argues that the decisive mistake was turning Aquinas's remarks on analogy into a theory. See chapter 5 of *Domestication*. Colin Gunton argues that the decisive mistake is an overly philosophical *via negativa*—a negative theological method that finds itself captive to a reigning cosmology. Whereas Aquinas's cosmology was compatible with the God of Christian faith, the rise of a mechanistic cosmology in the early modern period pushes God beyond all language and knowing. "Kant is the fate of the negative theology transposed into a mechanistic world" (*Act and Being*, 53).

23. Catherine Mowry LaCugna, "God in Communion with Us—The Trinity," in LaCugna, ed., *Freeing Theology: The Essentials of Theology in Feminist Perspective* (San Francisco: HarperCollins, 1993), 101.

24. Placher, *Domestication*, 7; see his discussion of postmodern theology, 7–17.

25. Ibid., 16.

26. Placher uses these words specifically of the work of Gordon Kaufman, but means them more generally for a theological functionalism that "has grown so widespread that in some quarters it grows hard to explain that there might be an alternative to it" (Ibid., 15). This functionalism exists on both left and right; it is never confined to what "those liberals" or "those conservatives" are doing. He notes that ". . . it is too easy for more conservative Christians to fulminate against the functionalist strategies they perceive among feminists or other theologians of liberation. 'Those people,' they say, are distorting the gospel to serve their own agendas—as if the God of American nationalism or free-market capitalism or male hegemony were not at least as much the product of theological functionalism and therefore equally a form of idolatry" (Ibid., 16).

27. Ibid., 17. To which I would add, "if we are to escape worshiping ourselves."

28. Nicholas Lash says "It is taken for granted, in sophisticated circles, that no one worships God these days except the reactionary and the simple-minded. This innocent self-satisfaction tells us little more, however, than that those exhibiting it do not name as 'God' the gods they worship." Nicholas Lash, *The Beginning and the End of Religion* (Cambridge: Cambridge University Press, 1996), 49.

29. Of course, my claims about analogy continue to apply. The full meaning of one, holy, et cetera lies with God, not with us. The church is one, holy, catholic, and apostolic analogically rather than univocally.

30. Ulrich Mauser, "One God Alone: A Pillar of Biblical Theology," *Princeton Seminary Bulletin* 12.3 (1991): 255–65; 256.

31. As Ulrich Mauser says, "The oneness of God and the totality of devotion expected from his human witnesses are only two sides of the same coin." Mauser, "One God Alone," 262.

32. See Marva Dawn, *Keeping the Sabbath Wholly: Ceasing, Resting, Embracing, Feasting* (Grand Rapids: Eerdmans, 1989), and Dorothy Bass, *Receiving*

the Day: Christian Practices for Opening the Gift of Time (San Francisco: Jossey-Bass, 2000), for further suggestions on Sabbath keeping. Though there are numerous other practices that enact God's holiness, I will only allude to them here: baptism as death and resurrection enacts God's judgment on sin and God's call for holiness; reading and proclaiming Holy Scripture invites the baptized to be "set apart" by finding their lives "set within" God's story; the way various churches practice confessing sin always implicitly recognizes sin in light of God's holiness and experiences God's forgiveness as the grace of being made holy as God is holy.